D1569429

The International Debt Game

The
International Debt Game

Brian Kettell, M.Sc (Econ)
Senior Lecturer, City of London Polytechnic

George Magnus, M.Sc (Econ)
Chief International Economist, Laurie Milbank

BALLINGER PUBLISHING COMPANY
Cambridge, Massachusetts
A Subsidiary of Harper & Row, Publishers, Inc.

First published in 1986 by

Graham & Trotman Limited
Sterling House
66 Wilton Road
London SW1V 1DE

First published in the USA by
Ballinger Publishing Company
Cambridge, Massachusetts
A Subsidiary of Harper & Row, Publishers, Inc.

© B. Kettell, G. Magnus, 1986.
ISBN 0-88730-117-7

Library of Congress Catalogue Card No. 85-28750

Typeset and printed in Great Britain

CONTENTS

PREFACE

Never in history have so many nations owed so much money with so little promise of repayment. Indeed the whole debtor/creditor relationship resembles a giant poker game. The stakes are the gargantuan debts of the debtor governments – standing at around $750 billion. This sum is nearly the size of the annual US budget and more than three times that of Japan's; it is $154 for every man, woman and child on earth. It has mushroomed from about $100 billion only twelve years ago.

This rapid increase and the difficulties in the 1980s of effecting smooth repayments have meant that the players of the game, the borrowers and the lenders have had to employ classic poker game tactics of bluff and counterbluff. The game has sometimes meant that borrowers were in bondage and lenders in growing suspense, neither willing to give much away and in most cases keeping their cards very close to their chests. Much of the debt may never be paid off, and a major default somewhere could trigger far-reaching political and economic consequences. These workings of the global economy have become a giant international debt game. It is a game in which the rules have changed, a bewildering situation for lenders and borrowers alike.

Over the last couple of years prominent world leaders have voiced concern about the situation. The risks according to US Federal Reserve Chairman, Paul Volcker are "without precedent in the postwar world". Says British financier Lord Lever: "The Banking system of the Western World is now dangerously over-exposed. If lending abruptly contracts, there will be an avalanche of large-scale defaults that will inflict damage on world trade and on the political and economic stability of both borrowing and lending countries".

The financial community, says Rimmer de Vries, chief international economist of New York's Morgan Guaranty Trust Co., is "in a historic period. There is a lot of worry that things could get out of hand". Dennis Healey, former British Chancellor of the Exchequer, warns, "The risk of a major default triggering a chain reaction grows every day".

The risks are particularly high for the largest American banks. At the end of 1983 the seven largest US banks (see below) had lent on average 137% of their capital to four countries alone: Argentina, Brazil, Mexico and Venezuela. With limited probabilities of being repaid the banks are risking depositors' funds when they should, according to strict banking principles, be restricting their risk-taking to shareholders' funds. Couple this with the fact that recent reschedulings of payments from Latin America involved more than 1,400 separate banks and one can appreciate how complex the international debt game has become.

US bank exposure to Latin America

Bank	Argentina	Brazil	Mexico	Venezuela	Total	Loans as % of capital
Citicorp	1,090	4,700	2,900	1,500	10,190	154.3
Bank America	300	2,484	2,741	1,614	7,139	116.7
Manufacturers Hanover	1,321	2,130	1,915	1,084	6,450	200.3
Chase Manhattan	775	2,560	1,553	1,226	6,114	136.5
J.P. Morgan	741	1,785	1,174	464	4,164	102.9
Chemical	370	1,276	1,414	776	3,836	136.0
Bankers Trust	230	743	1,286	436	2,695	119.4

Exposure (= outstanding loans) of seven large US banks to Latin American debtors at 31 December 1983, in millions of US dollars.
Sources: Keefe, Bruyette & Woods Inc

The *crisis* of international indebtedness occurred in August 1982 when Mexico, a country with some $80 billion of foreign obligations, declared unilaterally a temporary moratorium on debt payments. Several other major debtor nations were soon to follow suit in either suspending their debt service obligations and/or requesting a combination of large-scale rescheduling of their foreign debts and "new" loans from international banks and official financial institutions.

Since that time, what has been referred to as the debt crisis has been less of a crisis in the strictest definition of the word than a long, drawn-out effort, involving commercial banks, central banks, governments and official financial institutions, to contain the economic and financial fall-out from the situation and manage a return to normal relationships between creditor and debtor nations. There have been successful reschedulings coupled with changes in economic policies that have stabilized and indeed, improved, the debt situation for some countries. Furthermore, a strong economic recovery in 1984 in the USA, accompanied by a large increase in world trade and a modest decline in world interest rates have improved the external environment for all non oil-producing less developed countries. The decline and prospective weakness in oil prices, however, have given rise to new financial problems for oil-producing countries and their creditors.

Nevertheless, the makings of a future debt crisis continue to be present. It is by no means inconceivable that the world economy may experience another recession in the next two to three years. Furthermore, it is difficult to see the external environment for debtor countries, as regards interest rates and protectionist trade policies, improving rapidly. The effect of this is that it becomes distinctly inappropriate to extrapolate the favourable economic conditions that developed in 1983-1984 into the late 1980s and beyond.

The players in the game, moreover, may all continue to face problems in playing the current rules of the game. Domestic political unrest in some debtor countries in response to the impact of austere economic adjustment policies may cause some governments to be replaced by groups more hostile to foreign creditors. Some nations may just become reluctant to continue paying out more in debt service than they receive in new loans.

Banks may continue to avoid all but the best risks in terms of sovereign lending and financing, not least because of profound loan problems in their domestic economies and because of strong pressures to increase their capital and reserves. International institutions may continue to lack adequate resources and power to play a more substantial role and governments may procrastinate when it comes to reform of the international financial system. Any or all of these may contribute to a future debt crisis in which one or more countries withdraw effectively from the "game" or the international financial system. The adverse effects would be felt by banks initially but by all of us eventually.

At the very least, the withdrawal of or substantial decline in capital resources flowing to less developed countries, threatens a real and continuing crisis of economic development of major proportions. In the poorest countries, for example in Africa, a Malthusian scenario of population growth, famine and war is becoming increasingly realistic. In more advanced less developed countries, the shortage of capital for development and forced retrogressive adjustment may be accompanied by far-reaching social and political upheavals.

Finally, lest the richest countries be omitted, let it not be forgotten that banks, which lie at the hub of economic activity, face a future that is not devoid of opportunity but certainly characterized by significant risk. The same economic conditions that have contributed to banks' realizing problems in their sovereign loans have caused major difficulties in their domestic loans too. In the USA, for example, the Federal Deposit Insurance Corporation disclosed in 1984 that a record 797 banks were on its "problem list" after a previous peak of 385 in November 1976. The number of bank failures rose in the years 1981-1984 from ten to seventy (FDIC* – insured banks). Many of the problem banks had significant loans of questionable quality in energy, agriculture and real estate as well as in their foreign portfolios.

It is true to say that US banking problems are more domestic than foreign in that foreign losses at banks in 1983 were around $31 per $10,000 of loans, whereas domestic losses were some $75 per $10,000 of loans. However, banks seem to have realized domestic losses and provisions earlier and to a greater degree than in their foreign portfolios and it is possible that some major banks are more exposed to a rogue sovereign debtor than to a rogue domestic one. However, it is probably easier to contain the effects on banks of poor domestic loans than it is to stop the chain flows of international loan losses.

In Part I of *The International Debt Game* we describe the rules of the game itself. This takes in the basic rules of borrowing and lending and highlights the concepts of capital adequacy in banking

---

*Federal Deposit Insurance Co-operation, which in conjunction with the Federal Reserve and the Office of the Comptroller of the Currency, supervises and regulates the banking system.

and of solvency and liquidity. The origins and impact of financial crises are discussed as well as an early history of sovereign nation defaults. The section concludes with an appraisal of developments in the 1970s and 1980s in which the rules of the game underwent significant changes.

Part II focuses on the major players: international commercial banks, governments and official institutions. We describe here the rôle of each player and changes in their behaviour and attitude towards international financial relationships.

Part III revisits the game discussing the impact of a significant change in the rules which took place during the 1970s and early 1980s. Special emphasis here is given to describing the radical change in the external environment faced by less developed countries which was induced by major economic policy changes in industrial countries.

Part IV discusses debt rescheduling and the danger of default for both borrowers and lenders. We then outline various scenarios for the future, focusing on schemes involving piecemeal adjustment or wholescale reform. We conclude with some observations about the future environment in which the debt game will unfold.

November 1985   B. Kettell

                                                      G. Magnus

This book is dedicated by Brian Kettell to Lesley Anne Robb and by George Magnus to Briar, Daniel and Jonathan

ACKNOWLEDGMENTS

The authors would like to thank the following for permission to quote from their previously published works:

Professor Bordo, University of South Carolina; Professor R. Dale, Rothschilds; Dr. S. Griffith-Jones, University of Sussex; Dr. S. Heffernan, City University Business School; M. Y. Laulan, Crédit Municipal de Paris.

In addition they would like to thank the following for their valuable comments:

Mr. S. Bell, Morgan Grenfell; Mr. G. De Kiss, Chase Manhattan Bank; Mr. G.E.J. Dennis, James Capel; Mr. R. O'Brien American Express International Bank.

POKER

A card game for two or more persons, each of whom bets on the value of his hand and may win by holding the strongest hand on agreed system of ranking, or by bluffing others into choosing to compete.

We hope you can enjoy observing the game without losing your nerve before the end.

Good luck.

Part I
The Game

Chapter 1

The Rules of the Game

In the wake of the so-called debt crisis that erupted during 1982 and 1983, there followed a number of often acrimonious and frequently political exchanges between some debtor countries, credit institutions and a plethora of observers and commentators about where and how blame should be apportioned. The level of debate subsequently became rather more constructive as the players worked hard to restore some order to international financial relations and establish new rules. But what are the rules of the game?

The first rules are those pertaining to the activities of borrowing and lending. In a normal relationship between a creditor and debtor, certain financial rules need to be followed and respected so that both parties derive benefits from entering into that relationship. In the context of international lending, these rules were generally followed until the early 1970s. Thereafter, the key lending criteria of creditworthiness and the rate of return on lending became diluted by other lending and borrowing motives, which we explore in Parts II and III. However, in this chapter, we will focus on three factors. Firstly, we look at the concept of the basic rules of borrowing and lending and particularly at the capital adequacy of banks since one of the main repercussions of the debt crisis was to highlight the vulnerability of banks to losses as a result of having allowed their capital resources to shrink to dangerous levels. Secondly, we look at the non-financial rules that comprise the overall economic environment in which the game is played – these rules are at least as important as the more rigid and sometimes legally enforceable financial rules because they affect the willingness or ability of players to conform to the latter.

3

Thirdly, we introduce the concepts of solvency and liquidity since a distinction between the two is, at least in theory, important in dealing with problems that arise in relationships between debtors and creditors. This issue is explored further in Chapter 2.

Borrowing and lending are essential, efficient and desirable forms of economic activity that bring together individuals, corporate entities and governments for the purpose of intermediating imbalances or irregularities in the demand for and supply of finance. All parties should benefit: the lender takes a risk for which he expects to be compensated while the borrower finds it more productive to pay that compensation in order to acquire a wealth-creating or wealth-enhancing asset than not to pay it and forego both the loan and the asset. This is as true in international lending as it is for mortgage lending or any other type of domestic lending. Legal agreements stipulate the obligations of both borrowers and lenders and are designed to protect either party from unilateral actions that the other might take. However, these rules are only rules in the strictest sense of the word.

There are other rules, however, that are less specific, not legally enforceable, often more prudent and, in the case of external or environmental rules, not even within the authority of either party to control. These rules or conventions, as they might be called also, rest on confidence: the confidence that each party places in the other and that both parties place in the likelihood that the future economic and political environment in which they manage their agreements will, more or less, resemble the past.

In the international debt game, these rules underwent major changes or were, temporarily, neglected, leaving debtor countries and creditor institutions vulnerable and weakened. It should be recalled that the uniqueness of the debt situation in the 1980s derives from a number of factors, including, the sheer size of the amounts of money involved, the extent to which bank capital is at risk and the fact that debt problems are no longer confined to individual countries, with few repercussions for other countries and institutions. It is a global problem in which the web of non-legal rules has to be redefined or which players must re-adopt in some shape or form.

BASIC RULES OF BORROWING
AND LENDING

In a successful financial relationship both parties ought to follow certain basic rules. A borrower usually has to demonstrate why the loan is required, that he has or will have the income with which to repay the loan and pay interest charges and/or that the loan will finance the creation of an asset which will generate a future stream of income out of which debt service obligations will be made. The borrower may also be required to offer assets against which the loan may be secured and which may be transferred to the lender in the event of a default. If the borrower can meet all these requirements and is willing and trusted to meet debt service obligations on time, he may continue to borrow indefinitely, replacing old or maturing debt with new loans or rolling over debt from one period to the next.

The lender's first rule, sometimes known as the iron law of banking, is "know your customer". Without such knowledge, the confidence and trust that underpins a financial relationship is likely to be low and to be vulnerable to sudden, adverse circumstances that might otherwise be negotiated and resolved. Having then been satisfied about the above requirements, the lender must have the insight and discipline to ask the appropriate questions of the borrower and arrive at an objective and realistic assessment about the quality of the borrower and the use to which the loan is to be put. In taking the risk of lending, the lender must price the loan to take account of the cost of funding the loan (deposits) plus the spread which is the reward to risk or profit, that is then distributed to shareholders and set aside to build up capital to guard against the risk of default. The lender's asset management and asset pricing policies must be supplemented by liability management policies. In other words, he must ensure that his deposit or funding sources are stable, cost-effective to collect and diversified by their maturity, i.e. he should not lend money for ten years if his deposits are all withdrawable at seven days' notice. If the lender follows these basic rules, he can remain in business, satisfy his shareholders, retain the confidence of his depositors and build up a network of assets that are spread across a wide spectrum of borrowers and projects.

Applying the basic rules to international lending

The major risk to debtor countries in international lending is that sources of finance, e.g. for long-term economic development projects, will suddenly dry up. The major risk to creditor institutions, specifically commercial banks, is the loss that may result from the default of a borrower. Before the 1970s there were isolated cases of countries that encountered debt service problems or repudiated their debt obligations for political reasons. In general, however, the international intermediation of financial flows worked smoothly and efficiently.

The prevailing consensus in international banking was that lending, whether within or between countries, was a function mainly of the perceived creditworthiness of the borrower and the rate of return on the loan.

If lenders and borrowers satisfied the conventional rules of credit, neither party would be likely to suffer severe financial problems or undue loss. The productivity and efficiency of loans were enhanced by specific requirements relating to gearing, the rate of return on a project, profit considerations and so on. The recipient agencies of loans could function efficiently if short-term credit were used for short-term purposes and similarly for long-term credit. General economic stability was supported by the existence of financial rules. If lending criteria had been random or inconsistent, the result would have been greater uncertainty and increased volatility of expectations, which would have depressed investment spending and future economic growth. These financial rules were, indeed, the wheels of international banking because they derived not by decree or from government but from custom and usage. They were probably more useful than rules with legal status just because they tended to be more prudent and "common sense" than more rigid legal rules. It is no accident, perhaps, more than a decade after the first oil shock, that bankers' minds have turned back to the principles that guided their activities before the ascendancy of OPEC and the emergence of recycling.

Bank lending and the capital of banks

We have already noted that banking, which rests on confidence, requires lenders to build up capital to guard against the risk of loss or default. Capital adequacy is at the heart of banking for if the perception should grow that one or more banks were unsound, confidence might evaporate rapidly. If this were to happen in a local context, the effects on the community and in the wider economy could probably be contained. In a highly integrated and interdependent world economy, however, the risks of a collapse in confidence are much greater as are the difficulties of containment.

Bank capital

To most people, capital means ownership or equity, which is raised by selling shares or retaining earnings and its primary functions are to finance the purchase of fixed assets and to protect an institution's creditors. In banking, there is an argument that extends the definition of capital to include loan loss reserves and long-term debt. Loan loss reserves are earnings that are retained to absorb losses, so that if a loan has to be written off at some time, earnings will not be affected and creditors will be protected. Long-term debt would normally be payable only after a bank's depositors had been satisfied, so it too could be viewed as performing a similar function to capital, more narrowly defined. At the end of 1983, US banks' capital/asset ratio was 6.9% on the strictest definition, 7.8% including loan loss reserves and 8.1% including also long-term debt.

The purpose of bank capital is threefold. Firstly, capital provides a cushion to absorb losses arising on bad loans and allows a bank to continue operations whilst those loan problems are being addressed. Strictly speaking a ratio of capital to assets of, for example, 5% means that a bank cannot let its assets depreciate in value by more than 5% before it becomes insolvent. In reality, accounting principles allow banks to carry loans and securities at book value, rather than market value, so long as there is a reasonable probability that the assets will remain sound. Secondly, capital provides an assurance to depositors and other creditors that the bank can survive a period of adversity, pending the accumulation of additional capital from the generation and retention of earnings. Thirdly, capital should bear some relation to the degree of risk inherent in all transactions such as the risk of not being repaid in full or on schedule, the risk of a fall in the value of securities and investments and the risk of fraud.

Historical trends

In the USA, as elsewhere, banks' capital ratios have been falling for over a century. In the first half of the nineteenth century, total US bank capital averaged almost 50% of assets and by the end of the century, the ratio stood at 30% or less. In 1914, the US Office of Comptroller of the Currency (OCC) stated that banks should maintain a ratio of capital to deposits of 10%, since the major risk at the time was a sudden sizeable withdrawal of deposits. This norm held until the 1930s when the newly created Federal Deposit Insurance Corporation (FDIC) began to articulate capital adequacy in terms of the capital/asset ratio, again because perceptions of the time held loan defaults to be the greatest risk to banks.

Fig. 1.1. Capital ratios of commercial banks: USA

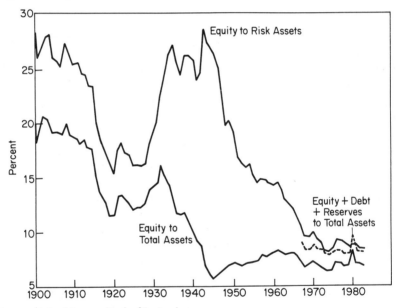

Source: Federal Reserve Bank of St. Louis.

With the ballooning of government debt, associated with the Second World War, banks acquired large amounts of risk-free Treasury securities (assets) and a new norm, the ratio of capital to risk-free assets, was established at 20%. This norm held through the 1950s, after which capital/asset ratios continued to decline again, reaching 10% in the 1970s. By the early 1980s, many banks including the largest were recording capital ratios of 5% or less.

Banks v. supervisors

It is appropriate to ask how and why this situation came about and what has been done to restore a greater feeling of safety to the banking system. To understand this, we need to discuss briefly the tensions that exist between bank management and bank regulators or supervisors. Banks choose capital ratios that maximize their shareholders' interests on the basis of a trade-off between risk and return. Pursuit of higher rates of return would involve, normally, higher risk and a reduction in the capital ratio (and vice versa).

Bank supervisors, on the other hand, set out to maximize society's interests. They aim to provide protection to depositors, to provide for a stable money supply and avoid financial panics, and to allow for an efficient, competitive and smoothly-functioning banking system. Higher capital ratios protect depositors and help to avoid financial panics[1] but they hinder financial intermediation by limiting the growth of the banking sector and increasing the spread between borrowing and lending rates.

Banks, therefore, do not take into account the social costs of bank failures in favouring lower capital ratios and the supervisors' objective of minimizing those costs lead them to favour higher ratios. This conflict is one of the reasons that capital ratios continued to fall, since there was no force of law to which supervisors had recourse. In the USA, this changed with the International Lending Supervision Act 1983, which empowered the Federal banking agencies (OCC, FDIC and the Federal Reserve) to set and enforce minimum capital requirements, as shown below:

Federal bank supervisors and proposed capital standards

Federal bank supervisors

FDIC – Supervises all federally insured state banks that are not members of the Federal Reserve System in cooperation with state authorities.

---

[1] Unless increased capital raises the cost of funds to banks which means banks may chase higher rates of return and, therefore, more risk in their loan portfolios.

Comptroller of the Currency – Supervises all national banks.
Federal Reserve – Supervises all member state banks in conjunction with state authorities, plus all holding companies.

Proposed capital standards

Primary Capital – The minimum ratio of primary capital to adjusted assets proposed by all three agencies is 5.5 percent.
Total Capital – The minimum ratio of total capital to total assets proposed by the FDIC and the Comptroller is 6 percent. The Federal Reserve proposes to gear the nature and intensity of its supervisory action to the zone within which a bank's ratio of total capital to adjusted assets falls.

Zone 1	at least 7 percent
Zone 2	6 to 7 percent
Zone 3	below 6 percent

Banks in Zone 1 have adequate capital provided the primary capital requirement is met. Banks in Zone 2 will be presumed to have adequate capital provided they are sound in all other respects. Banks in Zone 3, in the absence of extenuating circumstances, will be presumed to have inadequate capital, even if the primary capital requirement is met.
Notes:
All three federal supervisors regard the minimum ratios as a floor and expect most banks to maintain capital ratios above the minimum.
The three federal bank supervisors define primary capital, total assets, and adjusted assets identically. Primary capital is essentially equity plus loan loss reserves. Adjusted assets are total assests less intangible assets.
The supervisors define total capital, the sum of primary and secondary capital, differently. Debt with an original weighted average maturity of seven years essentially composes secondary capital for the FDIC and the Comptroller. All debt with at least five years to maturity, 80 percent of debt with four to five years to maturity, 60 percent of debt with three to four years to maturity, 40 percent of debt with two to three years to maturity, and 20 percent of debt with one to two years to maturity essentially composes secondary capital for the Federal Reserve, subject to the limitation that secondary capital not exceed 50 percent of primary capital.

Source: Federal Reserve Bank of St. Louis.

Reasons for decline

The decline in capital ratios was not always an indicator of greater risk in and to the banking system. A number of factors may be cited as justifying lower capital ratios. Firstly, greater economic stability, especially after 1945, with Keynesian demand management and the growth of the welfare state meant that banks had less need to plan for severe or worst-case economic scenarios. Moreover, the rapid development, deepening and widening of national and international money markets meant that banks could substitute, up to a point, access to liquidity for access to capital. Thus, capital, *per se*, became a necessary but not a sufficient benchmark for the soundness of banking institutions. Secondly, the formation of bank holding companies allowed also greater access to sources of liquidity which could be passed downstream to subsidiary banks as a substitute for capital. Thirdly, deposit insurance lessened the need to retain a given level of capital and reserves. Fourthly, inflation, which climbed continuously from the late 1960s until the early 1980s, was a major disincentive to the retention or increase in capital resources. This resulted partly from the tax treatment of retained profits and partly from the subsequent impact on bank share prices.

From the 1970s onwards, however, the tendency toward lower capital ratios could not comfortably be set against a less risky operating environment, which was being characterised increasingly by a decline in the quality of bank assets, notably sovereign loans, by deregulation and by increased competition. All three developments spelt increased risk for the financial services industry and contributed to the major concerns about capital adequacy and the soundness of the banking system.

Loan loss reserves

It has been argued that banks should have made greater provisions earlier in respect of their sovereign loans of dubious quality. The banking community, however, had little incentive to do so in view of the fact that all loan loss provisions have to be charged against income. With the onset of recession in the USA in the early 1980s and increased bank competition, bank earnings were already under pressure without having to bear the burden of large provisions, which, in any case, accrue relatively unfavourable tax treatment.

Table 1.1. shows the impact on the earnings of major US banks of having to make specific reserves against their loans to six major borrowers:

Table 1.1. US Banks: Impact of reserves on earnings

Bank	Total Loans to Mexico, Brazil, Venezuela, Argentina, Chile and the Phillippines (in billions)	Percentage Reduction in Earnings Per Share* from Establishing Loan Loss Reserves of:			
		1%	2%	5%	10%
Citicorp	$12.3	7%	15%	37%	74%
Bank America	7.95	12	24	61	121
Manufacturers Hanover	7.625	13	26	65	129
Chase Manhattan	7.175	9	19	47	94
J.P. Morgan & Co.	4.8	5	11	27	54
Chemical N.Y.	4.675	8	16	41	82
Bankers Trust	3.15	6	12	31	62
First Chicago	2.45	8	15	39	77
Continental Illinois	2.35	11	22	56	111
Wells Fargo	1.74	6	12	30	60

* Based 1983 earnings

Source: Becker Paribas

Since 1983, the regulatory environment has been tightened, especially with regard to the provisions of the International Lending Supervisory Act. The Act spurred the OCC, Federal Reserve and the FDIC to require specific reserves against sovereign credits which are subject to protracted arrears, non-compliance with IMF programmes or little prospect of an orderly restoration of timely debt servicing. Such credits are termed: "value-impaired" as opposed to "sub-standard", which is rather less serious; "loss", which means that the loan is uncollectible and "other transfer risk problem" which is designed to act as an early warning indicator. As at the end of 1984, value impaired loans had to be provided for by special allocated transfer risk reserves in respect of Zaire (75%), Sudan (50%), Nicaragua (40%), Poland (25%), and Bolivia (10%). The absence from this list of more major debtor nations may be explained by the data in the table above but, be that as it may, the overwhelming majority of major US banks has increased provisions – by around 20% in 1984 (see Table 1.2.).

Table 1.2. US Banks: key indicators 1984

TOP 15 US BANKS 1984

	Assets $ billion	Net income $ million	Change %	Loss provisions $ million	Non-perform- ing loans % total loans
Citicorp	151	890	3	619	2.4
Bank America	118	346	−12	861	4.1
Chase Manhattan	87	406	−6	365	3.4
Man. Hanover	76	353	5	395	2.9
J.P. Morgan	64	538	17	150	2.5
Chemical	52	341	12	165	3.2
Security Pacific	46	291	10	388	3.4
First Interstate	46	276	12	229	3.8
Bankers Trust	45	307	17	230	3.0
First Chicago	40	86	−53	465	3.0
Mellon	31	159	−14	117	2.8
Con. Illinois	30	−1,100	−	801	4.1
Wells Fargo	28	169	9	195	3.2
First Bank System	22	131	1	135	2.8
Crocker National	22	−324	−	527	7.1

Source: *The Banker* (Financial Times)

The rise in reserves at banks is attributable to two major developments. Firstly, despite an increase in loan write-offs, non-performing loans (on which interest is more than ninety days past due and which may not be treated as income) remain at high levels. Secondly, large additions to reserves and the issuance of preferred stock helped all banks boost their primary capital ratios in anticipation of the 5.5% minimum adopted by the FDIC in February 1985.

It seems, therefore, that the long secular downtrend in banks' capital ratios has been arrested and the banking industry is likely to become stronger in the future as banks' management strives to expand capital resources, either voluntarily or by "request" from the supervisory authorities and as the quantity and quality of assets come under increasingly close scrutiny from shareholders, stock analysts, management and supervisors alike. Sophisticated accounting practices can temporarily shield a bank's true balance sheet and have helped some banks on numerous occasions to report better or not-as-bad-as-expected earnings. The endgame, however, must result in more prudent reserves practices and tighter control over asset quality and asset growth.

Indeed, there have been suggestions that US banks should be required to observe an even higher capital ratio of 9%. This would require banks to make a major adjustment since half of all banks fall below this level, the aggregate being around 7%. To meet the higher ratio, banks concerned would have to raise about $50 billion in new capital or reduce assets and liabilities by around $520 billion — equivalent to a 29% rise in capital or a decline of over one-fifth in bank assets.

The Continental Illinois case

The deterioration in the quality of banks' assets in the early 1980s in respect of sovereign, especially Latin American, assets caused banks to suffer a reduction in earnings growth. It also threatened the international banking system with a major shock in the event that a sizeable proportion of those assets had to be written-off.

In May 1984, Continental Illinois, the eighth largest US bank, ran into serious financial problems that were not related directly to its less developed country (LDC) exposure. The events surrounding the banks' problems, however, served as a reminder about the precarious situation involving the adequacy of banks' capital resources and the exposure of other banks to those LDCs with the most serious debt problems. It was the revelation two months previously that Continental Illinois had $2.3 billion of non-performing loans, equivalent to 7.7% of its total loan portfolio and $500 million more than its stockholders' equity that caused financial markets to take fright and depositors to start a run on the bank that culminated in the largest bank rescue operation ever mounted by the authorities.

The bank experienced terminal damage in just two weeks during which time its share price fell to about one third of its book value and trading in the secondary market in its certificates of deposit collapsed[2]. In ten days in May, Continental Illinois lost about $6 billion or 20% of its total deposit liabilities. After the period March to July, about half of its maturing deposits were withdrawn or rolled over.

The rescue package provided initially for $4 billion of liquidity from the Federal Reserve Bank of Chicago and $4.5 billion from sixteen banks but the latter was made available for only thirty

[2] Certificates of deposit (CD's) are a key instrument for raising deposit funds.

days. The whole weight of the supervisory apparatus had to be brought to bear finally and provided for a $5.5 billion facility from twenty-four banks, a $2 billion capital infusion lead by the FDIC, a full guarantee of all deposits and other general creditors and a commitment from the Federal Reserve System to meet any extraordinary liquidity requirements.

The significance of the Continental Illinois case was, first and foremost, the commitment by the US authorities not to let a major bank collapse for fear of its impact on other US banks and, indeed, of the potential chain reaction in international banking. The second major impact was to cause other banks to take an immediate and in-depth look at the sources and uses of their own funds, i.e. whether they were especially exposed to any single group of depositors, form of deposits and recipient of funds which they on-lent. One by-product of this appraisal was to reinforce the tendency of international banks to reduce the size of, or at least growth of, their balance sheets especially as regards activity *vis-à-vis* other banks. That Continental Illinois' problems stemmed not so much from poor sovereign loans as poor domestic loans and a weak funding base was, in some respects, immaterial. The events of May 1984 demonstrated that a major bank could get into serious trouble, could probably not stave off a crisis once confidence had been shattered irrespective of the quality of management, and that only a major public rescue would preserve the institution, albeit at great cost to the shareholders and with a rather different and lower market presence.

RULES ESTABLISHED BY WESTERN GOVERNMENTS

The governments of industrial countries, chiefly those of the USA, Japan and the European Community, are vital players in the debt game, not specifically because of their financial contributions to economic development programmes and their interactions with private and official lending institutions, but because of the economic power they have to fix the rules of the game. International liquidity and the transfer of resources from North to South are essentially economic questions in which international lending and borrowing are but one, albeit important, part. The economic rules that derive from the economic and financial policies of industrial countries are critical to the outcome of the game.

In the 1930s, major industrial countries tried but failed to devise new rules to satisfy the demands for international liquidity that would facilitate the repayment of frozen and defaulted international debts and the lifting of related restrictions on trade and capital flows. The Great Depression destroyed the international monetary system that prevailed and the Second World War shattered the hopes for financial reforms and international economic co-operation.

However, the main proposals for reform, which included the establishment of an international monetary institution (later called the IMF) and the creation of an instrument of unconditional liquidity (later called Special Drawing Rights) were adopted in the post-war period. The Bretton Woods system, set up in 1944, played a significant role in the management and ordering of international economic relationship for about three decades.

After the setting up of Bretton Woods and until its demise in 1973, a high level of international co-operation helped to sustain world economic growth, the expansion of world trade and the integration of many LDCs into the more mature economies of the North. The system reflected the disenchantment of the pre-war period with the *laissez-faire* approach to financial relations.

Thus, rules were laid down for changes to currency relationships, for capital movements, for official sector trade financing, and guidance was given as regards the importance of maintaining a favourable climate for foreign direct investment from the North. All parties benefited from these arrangements, especially from the reduction in barriers to trade and capital movements. An important benefit to LDCs lay in the ground rules of the Bretton Woods system's provision for currency convertibility at fixed exchange rates and a multilateral framework within which countries could diversify their trade patterns and financial flows. This contrasted starkly with conditions before 1944 characterised by inward-looking trading and financial blocs led by colonial powers or industrial countries seeking hegemony. The move towards full currency convertibility allowed LDCs to run substantial and persistent imbalances in their bilateral trade and payments with large industrial countries. Thus, a country could run a payments deficit with, say, the USA and settle its dollar liabilities quickly and efficiently as a result of being able to convert other currency receipts arising from a payments surplus with, say, Western Europe.

Industrial countries benefited also in terms of the new non-colonial rules that allowed them to participate in the process of economic development and the opening up of new markets (through aid flows and foreign direct investment) and to continue having access on commercial terms to much needed raw materials and commodities. Admittedly, the relationship between western governments and LDCs remained weighted in favour of the former but there was, at least, a system, backed up by rules that permitted uninterrupted economic growth and the spread of prosperity.

Towards the end of the 1960s, stresses and strains began to creep into the international financial system. There were calls for a bigger transfer of resources through official development assistance, the creation of new regional development banks, a redefinition of aid and a new spirit to secure foreign direct investment flows.

The LDCs, in particular, looked for a new set of rules in view of growing misgivings about the impact of foreign investment on their economies, dissatisfaction with the structure of concessional finance and their difficulties in gaining access to the capital markets in major industrial countries. The debt game was about to assume a completely different and, eventually, threatening form.

SOLVENCY AND LIQUIDITY PROBLEMS

In a narrow, domestic context, a company may go bankrupt for either solvency or liquidity reasons. In the case of a liquidity problem, an ordinary company would find that the maturity structure of its assets and liabilities were so mismatched that it could not meet a significant withdrawal of its short-term credit lines. It might not be able to realize a fair value for its assets immediately though, in time, it could probably do so. The company could probably persuade its creditors to refinance its debt or lend new – cheaper – money to help repay older – more expensive – debt. The exception might be if the company were experiencing such large losses that creditors shied away from putting up any new money.

The company would normally be able to borrow as long as new

loans added to the market value of the company and as long as the cost of the loans was less than the return to the uses of the loans. At the same time, the company would maintain liquid assets and unutilized credit lines. Such a firm would be perceived as less risky and have a higher market value than one which received a higher income. Thus, maintaining liquidity has a cost – in terms of potential productive assets foregone – but a benefit – in terms of higher market value.

Strictly speaking, a solvency problem differs in that the market value of a company's assets is exceeded by its liabilities. Such a company would also be facing a liquidity crisis since creditors would not be interested in maintaining or providing lines and the company would be bankrupt. It would be wound up and be forced to sell off its assets.

Let us now look at the counterparts of these problems as they apply to countries. After all, a country cannot go bankrupt in the above sense, but it may fail to repay its debt or fail to meet its debt-service obligations on time.

Both the debtor country and its creditors must understand the nature of these failures if their financial relationship is not to deteriorate to the detriment of all concerned.

A country goes through a debt cycle. The cycle starts with the acquisition of debt which starts to grow more quickly than national income (a rise in the debt/GNP ratio). However, the rise in national income is more than enough to meet interest costs on the debt. In time, the interest cost on the next loan will equate the extra income made possible by the investment of that loan and debt will grow at the same rate as the country's ability to service that debt. This is the point where more rapid borrowing should stop. Debt is repaid as it matures and new debt is acquired. In effect, the foreign exchange obtained from new debt finances the repayment of maturing debt and national income is growing more quickly so that, eventually, there will be net loan repayments.

If more rapid borrowing continued, debt would grow more quickly than the country's debt-service capacity; the cost of the last loan becomes increasingly bigger than the productivity of the investment which it financed. It is at this stage if not before for other reasons that the country would encounter liquidity problems as it would be incurring more short-term debt and running down its cash reserves and unused credit in order to keep up its debt-service obligations.

To the extent that a distinction between solvency and liquidity is valid and useful, a country may experience a solvency problem in the final stage above, i.e. when the real interest rate exceeds the rate of economic growth. As a result solvency problems tend to occur gradually and over time. Liquidity problems, on the other hand, may occur more frequently and at random owing to sudden changes in reserves, the exchange rate, or the terms of trade. These concepts are explored in more detail in the next chapter.

Chapter 2
Financial Crises: How They Start and Why They are Important

The growing concern that the world financial system has grown increasingly fragile combined with the growing indebtedness of the less developed countries have increased the probability of a shock to the system. But one must ask why should shocks create problems? After all, in most industries, when people want to avoid risk they can buy insurance at an actuarially-determined price. Private firms willingly supply such insurance because normal economic and natural risks are statistically independent and therefore diversifiable in nature. However, as Dean and Giddy have illustrated, when one bank has problems the ordinary depositor does not have the information to distinguish isolated from general problems and may remove his deposits from the whole banking system.[1] In this way the economy can be disrupted at the expense of the public as a whole via a breakdown of the whole banking system. What may be perfectly rational and cautious behaviour at the individual level may be irrational from the public viewpoint. As Dean and Giddy emphasize, banking confidence is a "public good". So why does the public perceive banking problems in this way? Historically, most bank failures stem from shocks that are unique to an individual bank or some group of banks. If we get poor service from a restaurant we do not stop going to restaurants – we simply move to a better restaurant. Yet when banks appear untrustworthy we withdraw our deposits from all banks and go very liquid. The difference is that a single bank having problems may be suggestive that many banks are also

[1] J. W. Dean and I. Giddy, *Averting International Banking Crises* (Graduate School of Business, Columbia University: Research Working Paper No. 405A).

20

suffering and so an isolated individual with inadequate information acts on a safety-first basis.

The liquidity of a bank depends on not everyone withdrawing deposits immediately. When an individual withdraws a deposit, the risk of illiquidity, which would prevent others from withdrawing their deposits, rises. This means that confidence (and lack of confidence) in an individual bank is self-feeding. But what is it that causes financial crises to unfold and what are the consequences of these developments for society as a whole?

There are *two* main approaches to understand the role and importance of financial crises. The approach of Friedman and Schwartz[2] and Cagan[3] identifies financial crises with banking panics viewing them as largely unrelated to previous movements in economic activity. Banking panics in turn aggravate the effects of monetary contraction on economic activity. The second approach, following the seminal work of Fisher[4] views financial crises as part of the normal functioning of the business cycle, and explains them as a natural consequence of "financial fragility" and "overindebtedness".

Monetarist approach to financial crises[5]

Friedman and Schwartz in *A Monetary History of the United States* emphasize the impact of banking crises in engendering monetary instability. They illustrate that during the one hundred years studied the United States had six severe economic contractions, of which four were marked by major banking or monetary disturbances.

Banking panics, Friedman and Schwartz claim, arise out of the loss of confidence by the public in their ability to convert deposits into cash. In this case a loss of confidence would be typically precipitated by the failure of some important financial institution. As the panic spreads massive bank failures take place. Such failures

---

[2] M. Friedman and A. J. Schwartz, *A Monetary History of the United States, 1867–1960* (Princeton, 1963).
[3] P. Cagan, *Determinants and Effects of Changes in the Stock of Money* (New York, 1965).
[4] I. Fisher, *Booms and Depressions* (New York, 1932).
[5] This section draws extensively on a conference held at City University Business School in October 1983 and, in particular, reference is made to papers presented by M. D. Bordo and S. Heffernan.

are the consequence of otherwise sound banks being forced into insolvency by a fall in the value of their assets induced by a mass scramble for liquidity. So a liquidity crisis results in a solvency crisis.

The theoretical distinctions between a liquidity crisis and a solvency crisis are, in practice, difficult to separate or keep distinct. In the first place, a liquidity crisis might lead to a rise in interest rates as banks scrambled to raise cash from investors or depositors who sought safer financial or real instruments. Credit supply would be restricted and this would cause knock-on liquidity problems for even the most reputable borrowers. In the next phase, borrowers would try to realize at least some of their assets at distress prices, thereby forcing prices down against themselves. As asset prices fell, solvency would become increasingly threatened. This is, in fact, what happened in the famous collapse of 1931 of the Austrian bank, *Credit-Anstalt*. The bank was not insolvent but it declared a loss of 140 million schillings which was just over three times its capital. Although capital was sufficient to meet all the bank's creditors, it was unable to obtain emergency bridging finance and a run on the bank by depositors caused a financial panic which spread rapidly to Germany, Britain and then the USA.

The Fisher Minsky-Kindleberger approach to financial crises

In sharp contrast to the monetarist approach, financial crises can be seen as an essential part of the upper turning point of the business cycle – as a necessary consequence of the "excesses" of the previous boom. The modern proponents of this view, Minsky and Kindleberger[6] basically extend the views Irving Fisher expressed in *Booms and Depressions in 1932.*

According to Fisher[7] the business cycle is explained by two key factors: overindebtedness and deflation.

"Disturbances in these two factors – debt and the purchasing

[6] H. P. Minsky, "The Financial Instability Hypothesis: A Re-statement", *Discussion Paper* No. 7, *Confederazione-Generale dell' Industria Italiana* (Rome, 1979); C. P. Kindleberger, *Manias, Panics and Crashes: A History of Financial Crises* (New York, 1978)
[7] I. Fisher, "The Debt Deflation Theory of Great Depressions", *Econometrica* (1933), pp. 337–57.

power of the monetary unit – will set up serious disturbances in all, or nearly all, other economic variables. On the other hand, if debt and deflation are absent, other disturbances are powerless to bring a crisis comparable in severity to those of 1837, 1873, or 1929-33".[8]

The upswing in the cycle is precipitated by some outside event that provides new, profitable opportunities for investment in key sectors of the economy. Such "starters" can be new inventions, gold discoveries, or wars. The outside shock encourages new investment in these sectors with the result that output and prices rise. Rising prices by raising profits encourage more investment but also encourage speculation for capital gain. The whole process is debt financed, primarly by bank loans which, in turn, by increasing deposits and the money supply, raises the price level. An overall sense of optimism will raise velocity of circulation of money, fuelling the expansion even further. Moreover the rising price level, by reducing the real value of outstanding debt more than the increase in nominal debt, encourages further borrowing on the part of debtors suffering from money illusion. The process continues until a general state of overindebtedness – defined as "whatever degree of indebtedness multiplies unduly the chances of becoming insolvent"[9] – is reached. A state of overindebtedness exists when individuals, firms, and banks have insufficient liquid assets to meet their liabilities. In such a situation a crisis can be triggered through errors in judgement by debtors or creditors. Debtors, unable to pay debts when due and unable to refinance their positions, may be forced by creditors to liquidate their assets.

Such distress selling, if widespread, then triggers a liquidity crisis that could in turn lead to a debt crisis, a banking crisis, and a deep depression unless the process is averted by intervention by the monetary authorities. Distress selling if engaged in by the whole community produces a decline in the price level because, as loans are extinguished and not renewed, bank deposits decline. As the price level falls the real value of outstanding debt rises and, based on the assumption of money illusion both by debtors and creditors, according to Fisher it rises faster then nominal debt is extinguished. Thus creditors see the nominal value of their collateral declining with the price level and hence continue to call

[8] *Ibid.*, 341.
[9] *Ibid.*, 9.

their loans, while the real debt burden of debtors rises so they continue to liquidate.

In a series of articles since 1957 Minsky has elaborated and extended Fisher's theory of overindebtedness and the process which produced it with his concept of "fragility". To Minsky what matters is not so much what is produced but how it is financed. He maintains that what causes financial instability is a process which involves rapid and accelerating changes in prices of assets relative to prices of current output. Eventually, this leads to liability structures that cannot be validated by market-determined cash flows or asset values and that this ultimately leads to widespread bankruptcies and debt deflation.

So, according to Minsky, as the economy proceeds through the upswing of the business cycle, the financial structure becomes more fragile. A crisis occurs when a fragile financial structure is shocked by some event that triggers a sell-off of assets in a thin market producing a sharp decline in asset prices.[10]

The greatest danger point is in the neighbourhood of the upper turning point of the business cycle, when the weight of speculative finance is at its height. Then, business and finance have become more and more dependent on making positions by the sale of liabilities. Earlier on, they would have used money or liquid and guaranteed assets. In more detail, three stages are distinguished in the move from asset-based to liability-based finance. Firms ensure that their anticipated revenues exceed their payments commitments. If so, they do not need large financial reserves and so remain largely independent of what happens to interest rates. Put differently, the value of their business unit would remain positive even if interest rates rose. The second stage is one of speculative finance. It occurs when firms roll over bank debt and commercial paper. In order to do so, they must place liabilities in financial markets. Once they have done so, the current value of their business units will vary inversely with interest rates and may become negative. The third stage is reached when further liabilities are issued to such an extent that anticipated revenues cannot exceed payments' commitments for a long time ahead so that the current value of such business units is negative. The solvency of such

---

[10] H.P. Minsky, "A Theory of Systematic Fragility", in E. J. Altman and A. W. Sametz (edd.) *Financial Crises: Institutions and Markets in a Fragile Environment* (New York, 1977), pp. 138–52.

business depends entirely on the appreciation of its assets. Minsky labels this kind of finance as Ponzi-finance.[11] So in times of rising prosperity, liabilities-based finance becomes more important relative to assets-based finance. In other words, finance which depends for its solvency on rising prices becomes more important relative to finance backed by current values. Ponzi-finance then becomes more important relative to speculative finance and speculative finance relative to hedge finance. Financial interrelationships become appropriately more fragile. Increasingly there is risk that the collapse of one business unit may lead to a chain reaction.

The key problem is that default occurs following rational lending when an unanticipated fall in income or an unanticipated rise in borrowing costs occurs. Before the Second World War the prevalence of fixed-rate finance meant that variations in financing costs, measured after the event, were determined largely by unexpected falls in prices. After the rise of OPEC (see later chapters) it was unanticipated rises in borrowing costs that mattered. Given the widespread increase in the need for external finance (principally bank loans) this meant that insolvency (i.e. negative net worth) occurred, which results in forced selling.

Default occurs following irrational lending when net income is not rising faster than the rate of interest. Lenders should not lend in these circumstances and borrowers should not borrow. Kindleberger follows Minsky's line of crisis analysis. As he puts it, "The system is one of positive feedback. A fall in prices reduces the value of collateral and induces banks to call loans or refuse new ones, causing mercantile houses to sell commodities, households to sell securities, industry to postpone borrowing, and prices to fall still further. Further decline in collateral leads to more liquidation. If firms fail, bank loans go bad, and then banks fail. As banks fail, depositors withdraw their money (this was particularly true in the days before deposit insurance). Deposit withdrawals require more loans to be called, more securities to be sold. Merchant houses, industrial firms, investors, banks in need of

[11] Ponzi was a promoter who applied the "chain letter" principle to finance. He offered relatively high returns to people who lent him money, and he used the proceeds of additional borrowing to pay high interest to his first lenders. The money, of course, was supposed to be invested in some remarkable schemes that yielded high returns. In fact, like all such schemes, only Ponzi and those who withdrew early were able to profit.

ready cash – all sell off their worst securities if they can, their best
if they have to. Prices, solvency, liquidity, and the demand for
cash – in German Bargeld, in French *numeraire* – are interrelated.
Not only banking institutions, as Sprague states, but households,
firms and banks are very similar to a row of bricks: the fall of one
endangering the stability of the rest".[12] The metaphor is a *cliché*,
but nonetheless apposite.

In 1979 Minsky predicted that the Federal Reserve would not in
future be so able to prevent isolated financial failures from
destroying the system, stating "Given the fragility of our financial
system we will soon experience another brink reminiscent of those
of 1966, 1969-70 and 1974-75. This time, however, big government will not be as quick or as able (because of international
financial relations) to throw money at the problem, as in 1974-75.
In addition, the Federal Reserve will be more reluctant to intervene
by increasing the monetary base and extending broad guarantees
than it was in 1974-75. The subsequent recession will be both
longer and deeper".

The consequences of financial crises

In the 1930s, individual bank runs helped to trigger a chain
reaction of bank closures throughout the economy. Such a reaction
had and may have several important results. Firstly, the intermediation function of bringing together savers and investors may be
severely hampered, resulting in higher real interest rates and/or
credit-rationing and thus less overall investment.

Bernanke[13] showed that during a financial crisis, output can be
effected in a non-monetary way through an increase in the real cost
of credit intermediation. The disruption of financial services
between 1930 and 1933 hampered the ability of the US financial
system to provide cost-effective banking services. With the rising
cost of credit intermediation, credit for certain types of borrowers
(small farms, firms and households) was severely curtailed or only
available at a relatively high price. As Heffernan[14] has shown this

---

[12] Kindleberger, *op. cit.*
[13] B. S. Bernanke, "Non-Monetary Effects of the Financial Crises in the
Propagation of the Great Depression", *American Economic Review* (June 1983).
[14] S. A. Heffernan, "Country Risk Analysis: The Demand and Supply of
Sovereign Loans", City University Business School Working Paper, No. 52
(1983; rev. ver. 1984).

has implications for the current international problems. Debt servicing difficulties have raised the cost of credit intermediation (as evidenced by the rising spreads in the Euromarket) and reduced the supply of sovereign loans to developing countries. The share of net external borrowing from private sources (for non-oil developing countries) is expected to be much reduced in the early 1980s, largely because of a reduction in short-term credit facilities.

A second consequence of financial crisis is that the attempted conversion of bank deposits into currency, given a fractional reserve banking system, may result in a sharp contraction of the money supply. This occurs if a banking panic causes the public to reduce its deposit-currency ratio, or if the liquidity crisis *per se* causes commercial banks to reduce their deposit-reserve ratio in order to strengthen their liquidity position.

In addition there could be a reduction in the velocity of circulation of money (i.e. people hoard rather than putting money into circulation for spending). This occurs if the threat to the liquidity and solvency of non-bank financial institutions leads to an increase in the demand for money or as a consequence of widespread bankruptcies if the crisis produces such adverse expectations to bring about hoarding.

Another adverse aspect of bank failures is that transactors may refuse to accept cheques, causing a breakdown of the payments system. This breakdown causes financial loss and disruption to businesses and individuals not directly related to the affected institutions.

Heffernan has also illustrated that another potential and significant cost of financial crisis is that international capital mobility would be seriously impaired. As countries often borrow for development purposes this inability would reduce future living standards. So the financial crisis is transmitted internationally.

Many of the arguments for international lender-of-last-resort facilities, discussed in Chapter 7 revolve around the implications of international financial crisis.

How crises are transmitted internationally

A default by one small country would be unlikely to cause major problems in the banking system and the world economy, though there would undoubtedly be a period of extreme sensitivity and lack of confidence, which it would take all the skills of central

banks and governments to arrest and reverse. Multiple defaults, on
the other hand, or even a default action by two or three of the
largest debtor nations, would leave a number of banks technically
insolvent. In other words, a single default or even several defaults
by small-scale debtor countries would lead to a situation in which
the size of a given bank's assets, relative to its liabilities, would
decline. Its net worth would decline and the disruption of its
earnings and income would leave it short of cash. Multiple defaults
on a large scale, however, might cause an absolute decline in its
assets relative to its liabilities. A shortage of cash would be only
part of the much bigger problem of being unable to trade unless it
were acquired by a competitor or nationalised. If several banks
were affected in this way, a major banking crisis and a collapse of
confidence would have far-reaching, adverse consequences for the
world economy. Many financial crises in the past 200 years have
occurred worldwide[15] although they have differed markedly in
degree of severity. Monetary and real channels have been
emphasized in two leading approaches to international transmission. According to the monetarist approach, financial crises (and
also business fluctuations) are transmitted internationally primarily through the monetary standard. Under a fixed exchange rate,
such as classical gold standard, a financial crisis in one country, by
reducing the money supply or raising velocity in that country, will
attract gold flows from other countries. These countries will in
turn suffer a contraction in their money supplies and a reduction in
economic activity. According to the real approach, crises are
transmitted primarily through commodity arbitrage, and changes
in the balance of trade. Monetary factors are treated as of
secondary importance.

[15] Kindleberger, *op cit.*

Chapter 3
Early History of Sovereign Nations Defaulting

An appreciation of the current international debt crisis can be gained by looking at historical developments. International lending, sovereign and borrowing, are not new. Davis[1] describes periods since the Middle Ages when "factors such as the growth of international trade and investment produced a variety of new banking institutions whose objectives, lending practices, market environment, sponsorship and structure were not at all dissimilar to the Euro-banks established in the 1960s and 1970s. He describes foreign lending and gives details of a number of banks carrying out the practice from the fifteenth and sixteenth centuries.

Similarly, bank failures created by sovereign borrower defaults are not new. Davis cites two cases in detail; that of the Medici Bank and the South German bankers led by the Fugger family. Established in 1397 in Florence, the Medici Bank was the most important of its time. Its London branch made loans to Edward IV for the purpose of obtaining permission to export wool. Eventually over four times the branch's capital was lent to Edward, and the cost of borrowed funds to carry these non-accruing loans coupled with the periodic defaults stemming from the War of the Roses, ate up the branch's profits, despite the fact that Edward won the war. The Bruges branch manager far exceeded his established limit to Charles the Bold of Burgundy – over four times the branch's capital was outstanding to the Duke at the time of his death. Invariably, these branch managers found themselves lending new funds to heads of state to recoup existing loans. The bank was eventually liquidated. During the fourteenth century the three

[1] S. J. Davis, *The Eurobank* (London, 1980).

most important families of bankers in the Middle Ages: the Bardi, the Peruzzi and the Accingshi, all based in Florence, were ruined by the default of Edward III. When they suspended payments most of the other Florentine banking houses went under. The decline and fall of the Florentine merchant bankers was followed in the sixteenth century by a similar era of dominance by South German bankers led by the Fugger family.

The Fugger Bank owed its ascent and collapse to the Habsburg family which it financed during the sixteenth and early seventeeth centuries. Direct loans to monarchs such as Maxmilian and Charles V were initially made on a secured basis for a one-year maturity at a rate of 12 to 14% *per annum*; these loans were financed by matching money market deposits on which interest at 8 to 10% *per annum* was charged to Fugger as a prime borrowing name. Loans for purely political purposes were common. In 1530, to elect Charles V's brother as King of Rome, the Fugger made a 275,000 florin eight-year loan at 10% interest secured by various official revenues with a front end fee of 40,000 florins.

The banks increasingly found themselves lending new funds to protect loans to the Habsburgs; collateral consisted of pledged tax receipts in the Netherlands or Spain which often were not forthcoming. Against capital (reduced by loan losses) of 2 million florins, loans to the Habsburgs rose to 4.5 million florins in 1563. After a series of agreed moratoria and official Spanish bankruptcies during which interest rates were reduced and maturities extended, about 8 million Rhenish guilders of Hapsburg loans were finally written off in 1650, thereby wiping out most of the bank's earnings over the previous century.

Richard Ehrenberg, writing in 1693 of the relationship between the Fugger Bank and the Spanish Hapsburgs, stated somewhat prophetically that it could be summarised "Lend not to him that is mightier than thou or, if thou lendest, look upon thy loan as lost".

By the end of the eighteenth century Dutch banks were lending money to the Russian aristocracy and to the USA for the purchase of Louisiana and transferring funds owed by Spain to Napoleon. In general, however, international banking activity concerned the financing of trade in grain, spices, textiles and tobacco.

The nineteenth century revolutions in transportation and communications – railways, steamships, telegraph, transatlantic cable, Suez Canal, Alpine tunnels and domestic telephones, to name but a few – provided a major stimulus to international banking. New specialist financial institutions evolved, for example, acceptance houses and bill brokers in England and *hautes banques* and merchant banks in Paris and Frankfurt, with the aim of lending to foreign governments and providing finance for public works and for the growing foreign trade within the expanding colonial empires.

In the nineteenth century, investors accepted easily the credit of a number of developing countries with virtually no international borrowing history. Bond buyers were tempted by the substantially higher yields available on foreign loans in comparison to their own national government credit. The general glamour and financial promise of far-off lands, combined with the respectability of sponsorship of the great banking names of the day and rates of interest which were often more than double the national rates, ensured a remarkably wide audience for such issues.

Investors were remarkably reckless, continuing to subscribe to Egyptian loans, for instance, when the precarious nature of the Khedive's finances were perfectly obvious to all sophisticated observers in Alexandria. In 1868 the viceroy of Egypt obtained £7 million in contracting for a debt of £12 million. The promoters turned a profit of £1.7 million. Yet even the £7 million had no chance of being used productively by the viceroy, who loved yachts and palaces, since it was used to refund floating debt. The bankruptcy of the Egyptian government in 1876 and the consequent repudiation of foreign obligations were inevitable under these circumstances.

During the foreign loan boom in London, which culminated in the near failure of a major merchant bank and a Royal Commission of Enquiry, a fraudulent promoter, George McGregor, even succeeded in introducing a non-existent Latin-American country Poyais, off the coast of Nicaragua, to a London merchant bank. The bank concerned was fully prepared to launch an issue for the fictional borrower when the ruse was discovered. As Davis (op.cit.) has illustrated, the peak of the foreign bond mania and the banking expansion which accompanied it was reached in the late 1870s, with England being the major participant. "No country was so willing as England to expand credit beyond the limits of commercial prudence".

Defaults on those bonds were not infrequent. In 1841-1842, nine US states suspended interest payments, and in subsequent years approximately one half of the US railroads went into receivership. In 1873-1874 alone, the governments of Honduras, Costa Rica, Santa Domingo, Paraguay, Spain, Egypt, Turkey, Peru, Uruguay, Liberia, Guatemala, and Bolivia defaulted.[2]

In the mid nineteenth century three nations, the United Kingdom, France and Germany were dominant in international lending. The general purposes and objectives of the major lenders were the same, but their methods differed. In Britain private enterprise was the mainspring of foreign lending but in France and Germany foreign investment was an instrument for the attainment of national objectives.

It must be said that the political designs of the French government were not unduly successful. The huge volume of loans to the Russian government for railway construction and to Turkey, Austria, Hungary and Latin America for armaments were ill-fated owing to changes in government after the First World War.

German lending prior to the First World War was partly inspired by the desire to increase the military effectiveness of allies in Europe and partly encouraged by the government in trade and service accounts. On the other hand, British lending placed more emphasis on portfolio investments with government guarantees, and direct investments with managerial controls. In 1913 aggregate British investments in publicly issued securities were $3763 million, of which 47% was located in the British Empire, 20% in the United States, 20% in Latin America, and 6% in Europe. Functionally, railways accounted for 40%, government and municipal securities 30%, raw materials 10%, banks, commerce, and industry 15%. The dominance of the United Kingdom as an international creditor is illustrated in Table 3.1.

The ravages of the First World War and the consequent failure of a large number of countries with major international loans outstanding brought to a close this era of cross-border lending. The fortunes of the French middle class were particularly badly affected by the default on Russian bonds to which they had substantially subscribed in the euphoria prior to the First World War.

After the First World War, the United States became the world's leading foreign investor. Net foreign assets held by Americans rose

[2] For a comprehensive discussion, see H. Feis, *Europe: The World's Banker 1870–1914* (New Haven, 1930).

Table 3.1. Main Creditor and Debtor Countries, 1913

	Gross Credits			Gross Debits	
	($m)	(%)		($m)	(%)
United Kingdom	18.0	40.9	Europe	12.0	27.3
France	9.0	20.4	Latin America	8.5	19.3
Germany	5.8	13.2	United States	6.8	15.5
Belgium, Netherlands			Canada	3.7	8.4
and Switzerland	5.5	12.5	Asia	6.0	13.6
United States	3.5	8.0	Africa	4.7	10.7
Other countries	2.2	5.0	Oceania	2.3	5.2
Total	44.0	100.0		44.0	100.0

Source: *United Nations, International Capital Movements in the Inter-War Period* (Lake Success, 1949).

from $3.0 billion in 1919 to $6.7 billion in 1924, $8.1 billion in 1929, and then declined to $7.4 billion in 1935. The inter-war period was a time of great financial and economic dislocation and provides the most recent experience of large-scale defaults of foreign debts. After the build-up of foreign lending that occurred in the 1920s, the economic depression and sharp decline in world trade in the early 1930s resulted in widespread defaults by Latin American and Eastern European nations. By January 1932, the problem was evident as defaults on a total of $2.6 billion had already occurred.

Table 3.2. demonstrates the magnitude of the problems faced by various Latin American nations. In 1931, estimated debt service costs for principal and interest payments were running at approximately one third of government revenues in Latin America, and totalled 72.7% of Bolivian government revenues.

Table 3.2. shows that, as a proportion of export earnings, debt-service costs rose sharply from 1930. This was principally because of declines in the prices of the commodities exported by these nations. Prices of coffee fell from 18.5 cents per pound in 1929 to 6 cents in 1931. Tin prices dropped 55%, from 45 cents a pound to 20 cents a pound in 1931. Sugar prices halved, going from 6 cents a pound in 1929 to 3 cents a pound in 1933. A general index of primary products indicated that prices fell 60% from 1929 to 1931. The result was a devastating decline in the value of exports for the countries which specialized in the export of primary products. From 1928-1929 to 1932-1933, the value of Chile's exports fell 80%; Bolivia, Cuba and Peru suffered export declines of 70% and Argentina and Brazil had declines in excess of 60%.

Table 3.2. Debt-Service Ratios

	% of Government Revenues	% of Export Earnings			
	1931	1930	1931	1932	1933
Argentina	36.9	18.2	22.5	27.6	30.2*
Bolivia	72.7*	13.5	24.5*	50.0*	38.5*
Brazil	25.0*	23.5	28.4*	41.0*	45.1*
Chile	32.2*	18.0	32.9*	102.6*	81.9*
Columbia	32.0	14.0	15.6	21.8*	29.6*
Cuba	NA**	6.1	13.4	18.1	22.4*
Peru	34.3*	9.5	16.3	21.4*	21.7*
Uruguay	NA**	9.7	22.4*	36.3*	31.3*

* Years of partial or full default on outstanding foreign loan
** Not available

Sources: Max Winkler and Maxwell S. Stewart, "Recent Defaults of Government Loans" in *Foreign Policy Reports 7*, no. 22 (January 6, 1932): 397; and Dragoslav Avramovic, *Debt Servicing Capacity and Postwar Growth in International Indebtedness* (Baltimore: John Hopkins University Press, 1958) p. 194.

Because of depressed volume and falling prices, the value of world trade fell from $34.3 billion in 1929 to $27.9 billion in 1930, $20.00 billion in 1931, and $18.5 billion in 1932. In such circumstances, governments lacked the foreign exchange to repay their debts, and even where debtor entities set aside local currency in the amount of their obligations, there were no United States dollars available to fund the external payments.

The key elements in the series of defaults by developing countries in the early 1930s were the collapse in world trade, the decline in the prices of their exports, and the resulting unavailability of foreign currency to meet external debt payments. A crucial factor in these defaults was the rapidity with which export earnings declined and debt-servicing ratios rose. It was not just a high debt-servicing ratio that made a default more likely, but a sharp and unexpected rise in the ratio.

Ilse Mintz illustrated that the most important single factor leading investors to be less cautious was the complete absence of defaults on foreign government bonds during the entire period. The absence of caution on the part of investors was described thus:

> "Their attitude may seem somewhat surprising since, logically, we would expect their caution to grow instead of decrease, with the distance from the last severe depression. Their awareness that loans are tested in times of severe depression and that the absence of defaults at other times does not prove that all loans are sound, should have functioned as a brake on the over-optimism of the public. The spell of the long defaultless period made them forget that during the 19th Century, every major downward swing of the business cycle caused the failure of governments and other foreign borrowers to meet their external obligations. Or, if the disasters of the past were remembered, they were discounted in the belief that modern economic policy was able to prevent severe depressions – a belief strengthened by the mildness of recent contractions . . . The bankers' estimates of risk were an important factor in the decline of loan quality".[3]

So non-default on sovereign loans is historically a recent concept. It was on the basis of the frequent defaults in the one hundred plus years from the Napoleonic period to the Second World War that led Leon Fraser, one time President of the Bank for International Settlements, to make the often quoted remark, adapted from Alfred, Lord Tennyson, that "it was better to have loaned and lost than never to have loaned at all". Sovereign debt was repeatedly repudiated until 1945 but only rarely since; North Korea and Ghana with the latter's debt finally rescheduled, being two cases.

Certain characteristics of the pre-1945 defaults need to be stressed. A key feature of pre-war credit markets was the predominant role of bond finance. Bonds were usually issued at fixed rates of interest with long periods until maturity. These bond issues were purchased by private investors so that when debt-servicing problems arose bank assets were not at risk. So as the debt instruments were held by a widely diversified group,

---

[3] I. Mintz, *Deterioration in the Quality of Foreign Bonds Issued in the United States, 1920–30* (New York, 1951).

countries experiencing financial strains would typically suspend payment for a time and when they wanted access to credit markets again would try to negotiate partial relief on their old debts. An interesting historical curiosity is that following the end of the First World War, Europe owed $15 billion in debts to the United States, which it did not pay. The US Treasury continues to accrue interest on this debt and this now stands at around $30 billion (1985). This debt has been conveniently forgotten by the Europeans.

When the foreign bond market reopened in a cautious way after the Second World War, only the most established sovereign borrowers were again to gain limited access. The days when international investors could be induced to purchase the obligations of developing countries were over.[4]

---

[4] For a discussion on the differences between pre- and post-war debt developments, see pp. 139.

Chapter 4

Pressure for the Rules to Change: Oil Shocks and the Transfer Problem

The interactions between debtor and creditor governments are highly political, the outcome of which depends on the leverage that derives from the economic power that either group may exercise as circumstances allow. Until the early 1970s, the relationships were firmly weighted in favour of creditor governments. Debtor countries had little economic power except perhaps for some political control over the operations of multinational companies established in those countries. In terms of governmental relations, however, there was little question about the dominance of creditors.

In 1973/1974, OPEC countries administered a shock to this very one-sided relationship, having realized belatedly that the oil market had been "rigged" in the interests of industrial countries. The economic shock of the quintupling of oil prices left Western governments concerned, vulnerable, and powerless. They were concerned about the severe dislocations imparted to their economies from the increased cost of energy, vulnerable to acceding to political and economic demands made by OPEC governments, individually or collectively, and powerless to influence the massive disequilibrium in the international monetary system. They lacked the resources, not to mention the willingness, to play the lead role in re-distributing surplus OPEC funds to the rest of the world, notably the LDCs. They were also anxious to avoid a more serious world recession by interrupting what the banks seemed to be doing all too well – recycling billions of dollars to the LDCs, allowing the latter to continue with growth-orientated policies, which also meant increased demand for the exports of industrial countries.

A second flexing of OPEC's muscles in 1979/1980 brought

results that were quite different from those six years previously. In fact, the 1979-1980 oil price shock demonstrated the limits to OPEC governments' power to fix the price of oil in their favour. The efforts made by industrial countries to conserve energy, develop and switch alternative sources of energy and increase oil production outside OPEC countries, were beginning to have a notable impact on OPEC oil consumption when the radical shift in economic policies, first in the USA but emulated elsewhere in the industrial countries, produced a recession which compounded the decline in demand for OPEC oil.

The impact of OPEC: the transfer problem

The transfer of capital from one country to another is a common process of international trade. Nationals in a poor country may wish to borrow the savings of nationals in a richer country. Defeated countries have, after a war, been obliged to make reparations payments to the victors. Companies in one country may wish to acquire capital assets or set up subsidiaries in another. All these are examples of capital transactions between countries. All these involve money capital in one country being transferred to another. All involve the transfer of real resources as well as money.

Whatever the method, a country imports capital only when it gets goods (and/or services) in excess of the value it exports; a country exports capital only when it sends abroad goods in excess of the value of its imports. In either case, the borrowing or lending country must experience changes in its balance of payments which are directly connected with the borrowing or lending.

For example, if a country lends $100 million to another country it means that the lending country puts resources to the value of $100 million at the disposal of the borrowing country. The lending country will have to free resources valued at $100 million in order to export them to the borrowing country, which will import goods for $100 million or more. To be successful, any long-term capital movement will have to be accompanied by a transfer of resources of equal size. This implies a change in the trade balance between lending and borrowing countries. The process of transferring the real wealth, inherent in borrowing or lending, is known as the transfer problem.

The transfer problem played a prominent role in connection with reparations payments for war damages. Such payments occurred, for instance, after the Franco-Prussian War in 1870-1871, when France had to pay indemnities to Prussia, and after the First World War, when Germany had to pay indemnities to France. In connection with the latter payments, a heated theoretical controversy arose between Keynes and Ohlin. Keynes argued that the demand and supply elasticities of Germany's exports, which were necessary if German reparations payments after the First World War were to be made effective, were inadequate.[1] As events turned out, Keynes was correct, but his reasoning was not. German export prices did not fall, because lending to Germany was extensive, permitting the expansion of credit and maintenance of prices – in fact helping to permit inflation. Instead of reducing prices of exports, Germany maintained them. On the other hand, the recipients of German reparations, chiefly France and Britain, did not permit an increase in spending. Instead, they used the reparations receipts as a means of reducing their own debt. As a result, the price-specie flow mechanism did not work as expected.

Ohlin, arguing as Keynes later argued in the 1930s, suggested that since Germany collected the funds for reparations payments through increased taxes, spending and income in Germany were reduced. He further argued that France and Britain would regard the reparations payments as an increase in their incomes, and on that basis there would be a multiple increase in income in those countries, and hence an increase in imports from Germany, making possible the real transfer of resources.[2] Although Ohlin's reasoning was logical, the results were not in accord with this scenario. US lending to Germany permitted German imports to continue at relatively high levels, and when such lending stopped in 1929-1930, the system collapsed.

Writing on the "Economic Consequences of the Peace", Keynes argued that since such reparations implied the massive transfer of real resources and living standards from a devastated country to its creditors, and since this was manifestly impossible under any conditions other than direct physical enslavement, the consequences were predictable and graphic: bitterness, hardship, ferocious political reaction, indignant nationalism, Hitler and the Second World War.

[1] J. M. Keynes, "The German Transfer Problem", *Economic Journal* (March 1919), pp. 1–7.
[2] B. Ohlin, "The Reparation Problem: A Discussion", *Economic Journal* (June 1929), pp. 172–173.

More recently, the transfer problem arose in connection with the increases in oil prices imposed by the OPEC countries at the end of 1973 and in 1979/80. One very important effect of this was that the increased oil prices entailed a drastic redistribution of incomes in the international economy. Before 1973, the exports of the oil-producing countries amounted to roughly $30 billion. During 1974 exports from the OPEC countries increased by about $90 billion to a total of around $120 billion. This very large increase in income for the OPEC countries was, for the most part, a pure redistribution. The increase corresponded to a decrease in incomes for the oil-importing countries. There was no large change in quantities bought and sold, it was only a matter of revaluing exports and imports at new prices. The decrease in incomes had to be borne primarily by the large industrial countries that imported the larger quantities of oil, but many less developed countries that imported oil were also severely hit by this redistribution of income.

The increase in OPEC countries' income was so large that they could not even spend it all. Out of total income of around $120 billion in 1974, it has been estimated that the oil producers spent roughly $50 billion, while they saved $70 billion. Three different groups can be distinguished among the oil-producing countries. The first consists of Saudi Arabia, Kuwait and the small Emirates around the Persian Gulf. They are all small countries, their joint population amounting to twelve million, but they have large oil deposits and they produce 48% of the current output of oil.[3] (They are known as low absorbers.) The second consists of four fairly large countries: Algeria, Iran, Iraq and Venezuela. Their total population is sixty-eight million and they provide 41% of the supply of oil. The third group of the OPEC countries include Indonesia and Nigeria, two large countries with a joint population of 200 million and only 11% of the current production of oil. (The latter two groups are known as high absorbers.)

The general line taken by the various oil-importing countries initially was to deflate. This created the severe recession that took place subsequently. There was some adjustment as the oil exporters increased their imports but the major development was

---

[3] Percentage shares of OPEC oil before the production and quotas disputes in 1985 which have forced Saudi production down to around 2·2–2·3 million barrels per day at mid-year, compared with a quota of 4·3 million barrels per day.

the expansion in international recycling as the world's banks lent the OPEC surpluses to the oil importers, and thereby helped to solve the transfer problem. The weaker economies were thus able to pay for the oil without too large a reduction in living standards.

After the second oil shock in 1979/1980, however, the transfer problem re-emerged in a rather different light. Initially, banks responded by continuing to supply funds on a large scale to debtor nations. As the environment changed, especially as regards higher interest rates, poorer export opportunities for LDCs and a stronger dollar, and as banks began to pull back from international lending, the anomalous situation arose in which debtor countries began to export capital to creditor countries and banks. In other words, debt service obligations exceeded the amount of new loans forthcoming. This unnatural and unsustainable situation for debtor countries adds a further and more difficult twist to the transfer problem and begs the question as to how more normal relations can be established. Before addressing this question, we shall consider the respective roles of each of the major players – banks, governments and official institutions.

Part II
The Players

Chapter 5
The Role of the International Banks

The growth of international lending

Though international lending grew quickly in the nineteenth century, even more powerful stimuli came with the twentieth century's innovations in radio, telephone, air travel, telex and satellite communications and electronic information systems. Nevertheless, after the Second World War, most international banking business was for the purpose of financing foreign trade in a world characterized by a shortage of US dollars and extensive import controls. It was not until the late 1950s that international banking really began to develop into a global industry.

At this time, there were significant changes in the US balance of payments position and a steady growth in foreign holdings of US dollars. It became more common for banks in Europe to provide dollar facilities for customers dealing with the USA and to solicit US dollar deposits. By 1958, a European market in dollar-denominated loans and deposits had become established. One of the important reasons for the growth of the so-called 'euro-dollar' market was the desire of the Soviet Union to hold dollar balances in Europe rather than in the USA, two of the first agents being Banque Commerciale de l'Europe du Nord – a USSR-owned bank based in Paris – and its London relative, Moscow Narodny Bank. There were other reasons: the removal by Western Europe in December 1958 of most of the remaining foreign exchange restrictions on conversion by non-residents of earnings in European currencies and the return to full currency convertibility. These changes allowed closer links to develop between dollar deposits, other foreign currency deposits and national money

45

markets. By the early 1960s, the eurocurrency market was a reality.

In the 1960s, national commercial banks began to set up networks of branches and subsidiaries abroad so as to be able to operate in both foreign money and eurocurrency markets. There were strong motives to build and extend a foreign presence that were related to national banking regulations and capital controls and to the rapid growth of world trade and multinational companies. US banks were restricted by the Voluntary Foreign Credit Restraint Programme (1965) in their lending to foreigners and were affected, in terms of lost or foregone market opportunities, by the Interest Equalisation Tax (1963) and foreign direct investment regulations. The number of US foreign branches rose from 181 belonging to 111 banks in 1964 to 699 belonging to 125 banks in 1973 and foreign branch assets rose from $6.3 billion to $118 billion. In addition, the US Regulation Q ceiling on deposit interest, meant that when domestic credit was tight and market interest rates rose above Regulation Q levels, banks turned to their euro-branches to attract deposits.

In a wider context, the increasing attraction of the euromarkets to banks and sustained growth in foreign currency deposits placed with eurobanks stemmed from some unique features of this market, including:

- the freedom from regulatory constraints;
- more advantageous interest rate terms and narrower lending margins;
- geographical spread of the market;
- relative freedom of capital movements;
- a desire to spread investments globally.

With the removal of US and German capital controls in 1974 (and UK exchange regulations in 1979), the integration of the world's most important domestic and external financial markets had become virtually complete. The term "euromarket" gradually acquired a variant, namely, "xenomarket" since this type of commercial banking had become global and a twenty-four hour-a-day business. If it was true that the banking crisis in the 1930s had been confined to a few mature economies, then it was no less true that the years of expanding business and trade in the 1960s and 1970s resulted in no small measure from the creation of a truly global financial infrastructure.

The international interbank market

The growth and continuity of international lending is dependent on the important international interbank market, in which banks lend excess funds, solicit funds for lending opportunities and adjust the maturity structure and currency composition of their portfolios. In the eurocurrency market, interbank liabilities expanded to account for nearly 55% of total market liabilities by 1982. The interbank market share of worldwide bank liabilities was even larger at around 65-70% and larger still in terms of international foreign currency liabilities, at 70-75%.

The interbank market was also the forum where a number of key features of international lending were innovated and developed, including LIBOR – the London Interbank Offer Rate, which became the standard benchmark for international loan pricing – and the syndicated loan, which allowed many banks to participate in international lending by sharing the risk and allowed borrowers access to a greater supply of credit. So-called Jumbo credits of up to $2-3 billion were not uncommon.

Whatever the benefits and uses of the interbank market, however, the fact that most banks rely on the funds onlent by several large banks facilitates and aggravates the transmission of any difficulties affecting one bank or a number of banks. The market, after all, survives on confidence and although banks place limits on their dealings with other banks to reflect risk, confidence can be – and has sometimes been – extremely fragile in the event of bank difficulties, e.g. the complicated business of retrieving deposits from a problem bank, replacing those deposits, re-depositing funds in only top quality banks or, for smaller banks, facing an acute shortage of liquidity in the market.

The collapse in 1974 of I.D. Herstatt of Cologne and of Franklin National Bank of California, together with severe foreign exchange losses in Lloyds Bank in Lugano and Westdeutsche Landesbank in Germany produced serious disruptions in the interbank market. Some banks had to pay up to 2% more than the lowest market rate for funds and a few of the biggest banks reduced sharply the number of other banks with which they were willing to place funds. The events of 1974 were not just a case of laxity in banks' internal control mechanisms that affected temporarily the interbank market – though there were certainly deficiencies in the mechanisms for establishing and controlling exposure limits to banks as well as to countries – they were the first real manifestation of the risks that banks were prepared to undertake and, some would argue, failed to perceive. The next major shock came with the seizure of the American hostages in Iran in 1979 and the US government's response in freezing Iranian assets held in US banks. When Iran subsequently failed to meet a regular interest payment on one of its ($500m) syndicated loans, the country was declared in default and lending banks sought compensation from the frozen assets amid great confusion over the US Government's legal authority to extend its jurisdiction to the foreign units of its domestic banks.

By the time of the second oil price hikes in 1979-1980, there was a body of opinion that had cause to warn about the stability of the international banking system. Up until that time banks' problems had tended to be reasonably isolated and containable. Now, however, commercial banks were to face an international environment which they did not anticipate and for which they were not well prepared. Moreover, it was an environment which was to become increasingly publicised and in which their role was to become increasingly ambiguous. The stability of the interbank market was threatened again in 1982 by both the world recession and the unfolding international debt situation. Banks with poor quality domestic or international assets found it difficult and more expensive to raise funds. Furthermore, as debt restructuring negotiations got underway, it became apparent that the foreign branches and subsidiaries of banks headquartered in LDCs had been raising short-term money to fund medium-term lending at home. When these banks found their access to interbank borrowing severely curtailed or eliminated, debt-service difficulties quickly became more widespread or, in the case of Brazil, actually precipitated them.

As a result of the increasing fragility of the interbank market and its higher risk perception, many banks that had been attracted to participate in the previous decade became reluctant to raise their international exposure or pulled out of the syndicated loan market altogether. These included both small- and medium-sized regional US banks and non-dollar based banks. Their actions created problems for the larger lead banks in international loan syndications which had to sell down new credits. As well as the risk associated directly with LDC banks, additional risk perception emanated from the problems that beset Continental Illinois Bank in 1984 and other major banks with large exposures to heavily indebted countries. These risks induced even the largest banks to cut back their interbank lines of credit and the cutbacks were aggravated by profitability issues and capital asset constraints imposed by the Federal Reserve. Specifically, because of growing concern about capital adequacy, banks have felt compelled to curb their low-return, balance-sheet-boosting interbank lending and so help to restore capital and profitability ratios. As a result, the interbank component of the eurocurrency market, which had grown by 26% *per annum* between 1976 and 1982, contracted for the first time in 1983. In the first half of the year, it declined by 2.5% at an annual rate, from $1125 billion to $1111 billion.

Bank lending to LDCs

We have traced briefly the growth of international lending into a fully integrated, global industry and looked in rather more detail at the development of and problems encountered in the international interbank market – the "engine room" of international commercial banking. We turn now to the question of how banks became so deeply involved in lending to LDCs, because if there is a single issue that threatens the stability of the international banking system it is the prospect of a default by one or more LDCs. Such an event could cause severe problems for one or more major banks and, ultimately, spill over rapidly into the entire financial system.

Lending before the first oil shock

Until the 1970s, banks' involvement with LDCs was limited to the provision of short-term trade finance facilities, a few term loans to governments extended mainly in conjunction with IMF stabilis-ation programmes and often with gold as collateral, and a few project-related loans. Most of the finance raised by LDCs was acquired from governments (official development assistance), the World Bank (for economic development projects) and, as neces-sary, from the IMF (for balance of payments adjustment pur-poses). As of 1971, less than one-third of LDC debt was owed to banks and much of that took the form of suppliers' credits. In the preceding years, banks financed little more than 7% (on average) of the LDCs' net external borrowing.

Table 5.1. Financing the Non-Opec LDCs 1968-1973 ($billion)

	1968	1969	1970	1971	1972	1973
Current account deficit	6.8	5.9	8.7	11.4	9.2	9.9
Net external borrowing	5.0	3.8	7.1	8.2	10.5	10.2
of which, banks	0.3	0.4	0.4	1.2	2.1	3.7
suppliers credits	0.7	0.8	0.7	0.2	0.3	0.3
other private sources	–	–0.1	0.8	1.2	2.0	0.5
official sources	2.6	2.8	3.1	3.3	3.6	5.1
IMF	0.2	–	–0.4	–	0.4	0.2
short-term*	1.2	–0.1	2.5	2.3	2.1	0.4

* Including errors and omissions
Source: IMF, Annual Reports

In the immediate years before the first oil price shock in 1973/1974, it can be seen from Table 5.1 that the role of banks in lending to LDCs was still rather small though beginning to become more important. Let us look at some of the reasons why banks and LDCs were beginning to form closer financial relationships.

Firstly, during and after the second half of the 1960s, a number of LDCs began to open up their economies to foreign investment and trade and generate rapid economic growth and investment opportunities. To support the dynamism in these economies, governments and the multinational companies to which they played host now began to require increasing amounts of foreign debt. Secondly, the growth of aid from official sources had begun to slow down and had, in any case, been redirected towards those LDCs with the lowest *per capita* income and the least flexible economies. As a result, the "better-off" LDCs turned to private commercial banks for more trade – and project-related financing. The fact that the gap between commercial and official interest rates was narrowing made commercial borrowing less unattractive and the fact that banks, unlike the IMF, could not impose conditions and could arrange loans rather more quickly made commercial borrowing more appealing. Thirdly, the rapid growth in international banking and of the eurocurrency market in particular, allowed the supply of loanable funds to rise substantially. More and more banks were becoming active in international lending – around sixty new banks a year started to participate including, it should be noted, many that had little or no experience in lending to

LDCs or managing country risk. Fourthly, the development and expansion of the syndicated loan market allowed more banks to become involved in lending to LDCs, to spread their risks geographically and to share in the perceived rewards resulting from the strong economic performance of the borrowers.

The banks were not passive agents in the formation of relationships with LDCs. It was part of a, perhaps informal, strategy to grow worldwide, to service their major customers in the developing world and to reap the rewards from an expanding economic environment in which LDCs were playing an increasingly important role. Though it was not the only concern, the drive to increase assets was the prevailing influence in bank strategies in the 1970s, but too little attention was paid to the need to adjust higher lending spreads in lending to LDCs for higher risk.

Lending from the first oil shock to 1981

The first watershed in international lending to LDCs arrived with the first oil price shock in 1973/74, which created a massive imbalance in the international balance of payments. The current account balance of oil exporting countries jumped from $7 billion in 1973 to $68 billion in 1974 and remained between $30 and $40 billion until 1977, while the current account balance of the non-oil LDCs deteriorated from –$11 billion in 1973 to –$37 billion in 1974 and –$46 billion in 1975.

Table 5.2. Current Account Balances 1973-1978 ($billion)

	1973	1974	1975	1976	1977	1978	1979	1980	1981
Industrial countries	20	–11	20	1	–2	33	–6	–40	1
Oil exporting countries	7	68	35	40	30	2	69	114	65
Non-oil LDCs	–11	–37	–46	–33	–29	–41	–61	–89	–108
Centrally planned Economies	–2	–2	–9	–7	–3	–5	–3	–4	–4

Source: BIS, OECD, IMF

At the time of the oil shock, there were dire predictions that the world would never be able to live with such large payments imbalances and that a major economic depression was likely since the oil price increases were seen as a sort of tax on the rest of the world that would not be offset by additional spending from the

OPEC countries. The IMF and World Bank did not have the resources to lend to the rest of the world and the governments of the industrial countries had neither the willingness nor the ability to take the steps necessary to help the world economy to adjust. Almost by default, international banks took on the job of recycling the surpluses of the OPEC countries to the rest of the world, notably the non-oil producing LDCs.

As it happened, OPEC nations did spend rather more than had been expected and, being for the most part conservative investors, they deposited substantial funds at relatively short maturities in the eurocurrency market. Private financial institutions now found themselves awash with liquidity at a time when there was a large-scale demand for credit on the part of LDCs and when mechanisms existed to intermediate those surplus funds to LDCs.

In recent years there have been frequent criticisms that after 1973/1974 banks "overlent" and/or that LDCs "over borrowed". Such criticisms are really rather academic and meaningless in the absence of qualification and are made with the benefit of hindsight. There is little question that the banks lacked proper tools and mechanisms for evaluating sovereign government risk and that LDCs borrowed partly, but not exclusively, for the purpose of sustaining consumption. However, had the banks not intermediated the so-called petrodollars in the way they did, LDCs would have been forced to curtail their development programmes sharply and economic activity in industrial countries would have fallen more dramatically and for much longer. That both of these situations developed in the early 1980s had less to do with overlending or overborrowing than with the radical and fundamental change that occurred after 1979 in the rules of the debt game which we will explore in Chapter 8.

The most important development to be noted in and immediately after the 1973/1974 period was the major change in LDC financing between private and official sources. Banks were now the most important players in the game, encouraged in part by the governments of industrial countries which, at the very least, did nothing to interfere. Multilateral official institutions, notably the IMF, became in effect the lender of last resort to LDCs if private markets were unwilling to lend or accept the risks involved.

In 1979/1980, the second oil shock generated new upheavals in the international economic system. The OPEC surplus rose from $2 billion in 1978 to $114 billion in 1980 and remained over $60

Table 5.3. Financing the LDCs* in the 1970s

	1971	1976	1978	1980
Total external debt† ($billion)	90	220	345	465
– financed by (%):				
Bank loans	12.2	29.1	30.4	33.3
Other private lending	10.0	7.3	8.4	7.6
Total private	22.2	36.4	38.8	40.9
Official sources	26.7	16.8	14.2	12.3
Multilateral sources	11.1	11.8	11.6	12.0
Export credits	30.0	23.2	24.6	24.5
Other‡	10.0	11.8	10.7	10.3

* Including OPEC
† External term debt
‡ Includes lending by OPEC countries

Source: OECD, Development Co-operation 1982 Review

billion in 1981, while the non-oil LDCs increased their deficit from $41 billion in 1978 to $108 billion in 1981. This created a renewed major demand for recycling, which banks duly fulfilled but this time the warnings of more serious problems were gathering. In 1979 Turkey was obliged to renegotiate its foreign debt and the Iranian crisis sent shock waves through the banking system. In both cases, however, the conventional wisdom was that these were isolated incidents and the result of specific domestic political upheavals. In the few years before the debt crisis finally "broke" bank lending continued at a rapid pace (see Table 5.4).

There are two important aspects of banks' lending activities in this period which need to be highlighted. The first is the concentration of banks' exposure among a small group of countries. The second is the steady growth in the proportion of

TABLE 5.4. Bank Lending to Non-Oil LDCs, 1976-1981

	1976	1977	1978	1979	1980	1981
Lending to all non-oil LDCs ($billion)	21	15	25	40	49	50
– as % current account deficit	64	52	61	66	55	46
Increase in bank claims (%)	28.7	14.9	19.3	26.6	26.2	22.2
Share of non-oil LDCs in total net bank lending (%)	30	21	28	32	31	30

Sources: BIS, IMF

short-term debt, i.e. debt that falls due for repayment within
twelve months (see Table 5.5).

From after the first oil price shock to just after the second one,
the outstanding bank loans to the major LDC borrowers[1] grew at
an average annual rate of 30%, compared with just over 22% for
all LDCs. By 1982, this group accounted for 84% of all debt owed
by LDCs to BIS banks. For US banks alone, the group accounted
for 88% of LDC bank debt owed to the nine largest US banks and
90% of the debt owed to all US banks. An increasing proportion
of the debt contracted in the last few years was of a short-term
character. This was deemed to be less risky than longer-term
commitments to which lenders would be "locked-in", but the
rapid growth in short-term debt increased the vulnerability of
borrowers to a sudden drop in the willingness of lenders to roll
over that debt – an ominous development that occurred in
1982-1983 – and it also made it more difficult for banks to extricate
themselves from particular debt situations on the grounds that if all
lenders withdrew credit lines, they would precipitate the very
liquidity crisis they sought to avoid. Mid-1984 data, however,
confirm that the proportion of short-term debt started to decline.

Lending in 1982-1984

The second watershed for the market in lending to LDCs can be
dated to early 1982, around six months before Mexico announced
that it could not repay its loans. A decline in new bank lending to
LDCs had started in the Spring of 1982 and it gathered pace as
banks reacted quickly and sharply to a growing loss of confidence
in LDC lending (see Table 5.6). Banks actually reduced their
exposure to Eastern Europe in the first half of the year and the
slowdown in the growth of assets to other countries followed
quickly as more countries experienced debt service difficulties or as
one country's problems became regional problems in the eyes of
banks. For example, the Polish debt crisis after 1981 cast a long
shadow over the whole of Eastern Europe as a credit risk and the
Mexico debt crisis had a similar affect on both Latin America in
particular and oil-producing nations in general.

[1] Twenty-one in all, comprising, Argentina, Brazil, Chile, Colombia, Ecuador,
Mexico, Peru, Venezuela, Indonesia, Korea, Malaysia, Philippines, Taiwan,
Thailand, Algeria, Egypt, Israel, Ivory Coast, Morocco, Algeria, Turkey.

Table 5.5. Assets by Amount and Maturity of BIS Banks
vis-à-vis LDCs. 1978-1984†

Mid-Year	Assets ($bn)	Maturing within 12 Months (%)*	1-2 Years (%)*	Over 2 Years (%)*	Undisbursed Credit Commitments (%)*
1. ALL LDCS					
1978	155.3	46.3	10.4	34.7	31.1
1982	343.5	50.0	7.3	35.4	20.6
1983	366.6	48.4	6.3	36.9	15.0
1984	383.6	42.0	7.5	41.5	36.1
LATIN AMERICA					
1978	83.4	41.0	12.5	40.8	24.7
1982	209.5	47.0	8.2	39.6	13.1
1983	217.9	45.5	6.7	41.6	7.6
MIDDLE EAST					
1978	26.7	67.3	6.2	22.3	38.4
1982	40.8	80.0	4.3	10.8	22.7
1983	39.8	78.0	4.8	10.6	21.7
AFRICA					
1978	18.4	30.3	9.6	32.9	36.9
1982	32.5	30.0	7.1	33.9	29.0
1983	34.8	30.7	7.2	32.6	24.1
ASIA					
1978	26.8	52.8	9.0	29.2	39.7
1982	62.2	51.5	6.4	37.5	40.1
1983	74.1	49.5	5.5	39.0	29.0
2. EASTERN EUROPE					
1978	42.5	45.5	10.6	30.6	23.7
1982	54.3	39.8	9.9	34.7	11.7
1983	50.4	38.0	10.2	36.4	12.3
3. ALL COUNTRIES					
1978	255.9	45.3	10.6	34.1	28.4
1982	506.3	47.3	7.4	36.8	21.0
1983	534.0	46.0	6.8	38.2	16.6
1984	563.5	42.0	7.4	41.0	17.5

4. MID-1983 COUNTRY SPOTLIGHT

Country	Assets	% Region	% LDCs & E. Europe	% All Countries
Argentina	25.8	11.3	6.0	4.8
Brazil	64.5	28.3	14.9	11.4
Chile	13.0	5.7	3.0	2.3
Columbia	6.6	2.9	1.5	1.2
Mexico	70.3	30.9	16.3	12.5
Venezuela	26.9	11.8	6.2	4.8
Total	*207.1*	*90.9*	*47.9*	*36.7*

| Mid-Year | Assets ($bn) | Maturing within | | | Undisbursed Credit Commitments (%)* |
		12 Months (%)*	1-2 Years (%)*	Over 2 Years (%)*	
Iran	1.6	4.0	0.4	0.3	
Iraq	2.0	5.0	0.5	0.4	
Total	*3.6*	*9.0*	*0.9*	*0.7*	
Algeria	7.1	21.1	1.6	1.3	
Nigeria	9.2	27.3	2.1	1.6	
Total	*16.3*	*48.4*	*3.7*	*2.9*	
Indonesia	12.5	15.3	2.9	2.2	
S. Korea	25.5	31.2	5.9	4.5	
Malaysia	9.6	11.7	2.2	1.7	
Philippines	12.6	15.4	2.9	2.2	
Taiwan	5.4	6.6	1.3	1.0	
Total	*65.6*	*80.2*	*15.2*	*11.6*	
Poland	9.6	19.9	2.2	1.7	
Romania	3.6	7.5	0.8	0.6	
USSR	15.7	32.6	3.6	2.8	
Total	*28.9*	*60.0*	*4.6*	*5.1*	
Yugoslavia	9.6	7.3	2.2	1.7	
Spain	26.6	20.2	6.2	4.7	
S. Africa	18.6	14.1	4.3	3.3	
Portugal	10.9	8.3	2.5	1.9	
Greece	12.5	9.5	2.9	2.2	
Australia	19.8	15.0	3.5	2.7	
Total	*98.0*	*74.4*	*22.7*	*17.4*	

Notes
† 1984 data, new and broader coverage but only for all LDCs and total countries.
* Per cent of assets, excluding unallocated
Reporting area/banks or BIS banks refer to banks in Group of ten countries plus Switzerland, Austria, Ireland, Denmark.
Source: BIS

Bank lending to all non-OPEC LDCs had risen by nearly $40 billion in 1981 but fell to $20 billion in 1982 and less than $12.5 billion in 1983, despite large officially-backed lending packages in conjunction with the IMF, designed to maintain credit flows (so-called, involuntary lending). Taking account of the deposits made by these countries, net flows slowed from $30 billion in 1981 to $15 billion in 1982 and barely $2 billion in 1983. If account is then taken of net interest payments due to banks, the ominous situation developed where banks became net recipients of capital transfers.

Table 5.6. The Slowdown in Bank Lending
1980-84 ($billion)

Banks' Claim on:	1980	1981	1982	1983	1984	End 1984 Level
All LDCs	52.8	45.9	23.4	20.9	8.1	482.7
Non-OPEC LDCs	39.0	39.9	19.8	12.4	8.8	329.3
OPEC	7.0	4.2	8.2	9.7	−0.6	105.5
Eastern Europe	6.8	4.8	−4.6	−1.2	−0.1	47.9
Latin America	27.3	30.5	12.2	8.6	1.3	211.0
Net Banking Flows 1980-1984 ($ bn)*						
	1980	1981	1982	1983	1984	End 1984 Level
All LDCs	−6.1	−36.2	−34.7	−20.5	21.1	−149.4
Non-OPEC LDCs	−35.1	−30.5	−14.9	−1.6	13.0	−158.8
OPEC	34.9	−1.0	−26.4	−23.1	3.7	35.1
Eastern Europe	−5.9	−4.7	6.6	4.2	4.4	−25.7

* Gross deposits (+) minus gross borrowings (−)

1984 data, new and broader coverage
Source: BIS

The key factor that caused the role-reversal between banks and LDC borrowers was the rise in interest rates. Firstly, high interest rates have effectively shortened the life of loans. Normally, maturing debt may be rolled over or extended or augmented for long periods before net repayments of capital are made. Even as new lending is taking place, however, a rise in interest costs can exceed a rise in loans. Thus, in a number of countries, a net outflow of funds occurred before any debt crisis emerged. As the debt crisis became more serious, banks did not roll over some short-term debts and, in some cases, did not replace maturing-term debts with new credits. For the largest twenty-four LDC borrowers, there was a net inflow of funds (gross inflows minus gross outflows, including interest) of around $25 billion in the first half of 1978. By 1981, the net inflow was zero and by 1982-1983, the average net outflow was around $15 billion. In 1984, non-OPEC countries in Latin America made interest payments on their foreign debt of around $30 billion, while banks' net claims fell by nearly $8 billion despite new loans in the context of rescheduling.

Uneasy calm in debt situation 1983-1985

Although voluntary lending to many of the most important LDC
borrowers had effectively dried up, banks remained partly
unwilling and partly unable to withdraw from this activity
altogether. They were unwilling to close the door to countries that
were managing to sustain a favourable balance of payments
position and to implement sound economic policies (mostly in
Asia). They were unable to pull out (though some smaller banks
did) of the most seriously affected LDC borrowers for fear of
precipitating the very crisis they sought to avoid and in order to
protect, as best they could, the assets already on their books.
Moreover, the slowdown in LDC lending must also be seen in a
wider context in which many countries began to pursue more
prudent policies and painful economic adjustment, with or
without the IMF, in order to stabilize or reduce the demand for
foreign bank loans.

Calm: Firstly, the recovery of economic activity in a few
industrial countries, notably the USA, succeeded in
stimulating world trade and the exports of the most
heavily indebted LDCs.

Uneasy: The recovery may not be sustained through the end
of the 1980s; interest rates remain high in real terms
and protectionist tendencies are increasing.

Calm: Secondly, the IMF played a bigger role in maintaining an adequate flow of funds to LDCs. The
strategy has been to negotiate with conditions an
economic adjustment programme, upon implementation of which a series of large-scale credits are
extended but to make such credit extensions dependent on the provision of "involuntary" funds by
banks. A more co-ordinated approach by the banks
and the IMF has helped to create greater consistency
between banks' lending policies and countries'
borrowing policies, and general economic policy
decision-making. Co-operation between the banks
and the World Bank in financing economic development projects has been welcomed also.

Uneasy: The dependence on the "IMF Agreement" as the
key to unlock the door to new comercial bank

financing is based on the IMF's ability to impose conditions relating to economic adjustment. By and large, the IMF Agreement is designed to restore financial stability, domestically and externally, initially by restraining domestic demand. This involves having to implement large cutbacks in imports, which means someone else's exports fall. The wider the application of IMF conditionality programmes, the greater is likely to be the restraint in world trade.

Calm: The debt reschedulings undertaken by banks (twenty-two countries and $60 billion of debt in 1983) were a vital first step, to the extent that they stretched maturing debt out some seven to nine years. Moreover, IMF programmes provided for $14 billion of new lending, of which $10 billion was drawn. Half of the debt rescheduling and two thirds of the new lending were in respect of Brazil and Mexico.

Uneasy: Debt rescheduling, apart from being extraordinarily time-consuming and expensive (the borrower usually pays), have been carried out on a case-by-case approach which has a number of weaknesses. (See Chapter 9.)

Calm: Finally, banks made independent moves to strengthen their financial structure by cutting back their short-term interbank funding and raising more longer-term finance, by reducing their low-yield interbank business and by trying to tailor their business activities to both higher-yield customer relationships and the provision of fee-based financial services.

Uneasy: There is no problem here except time and the continuing vulnerability of banks to a deterioration in the condition of major LDC debtor countries.

In March 1984, new disturbances arose. Argentina, which had objected to the IMF conditions as part of a rescheduling programme, had missed interest payments on existing loans. The significance lay in the fact that, under US accounting regulations, if interest payments are over 90 days late (in this case, 31 March

1984), the loans must be declared "non-performing", and cannot be credited with interest in the income statement.

Since the shares of US banks had already declined sharply, the financial industry was in the throes of being de-regulated and bank earnings were under pressure from numerous domestic and external sources, the banks did not relish the prospect of having to declare all their Argentine loans non-performing.

At the eleventh hour, four major borrowers, lead by Mexico (and including Brazil, Colombia and Venezuela) got together for the first time and seized the initiative from the banks in securing a bridging loan to Argentina. The four countries lent $300 million guaranteed by the US Treasury; the banks provided $100 million, secured by Argentine deposits at the Federal Reserve; and Argentina found $100 million in the reserves. This event was significant because Mexico helped Argentina circumvent the authority of both the IMF and the banks. The banks, in particular, had to retreat from their prior insistence that an IMF agreement had to be made before new lending could resume and, on the creditors' side of the table, the balance of political power had moved more towards the US Government and away from the IMF and the commercial banks.

When the June deadline fell due, there was still no IMF agreement and banks declared some of their Argentina loans non-performing. However, banks did lose some leverage *vis-à-vis* the Latin American countries and would have to continue to deal with a country whose new political leaders (post-Falklands) wanted to re-negotiate the previous (military) government's already rescheduled debt. If governments change and the willingness to service debt properly changes with them, banks could face even bigger problems in Latin America and elsewhere.

In any event, the major significance of the 1984 dealings with and concerning Argentina was the politicisation of the debt situation. Many LDCs began to have severe misgivings about the political impact of economic austerity and to question the costs of slashing imports and reducing living standards to produce external trade surpluses (which many LDCs did in 1983-1984) only to see them reduced or offset by interest payments on foreign debt.

Lending and borrowing rules in the 1970s

The concepts that guided borrowing and lending decisions in the 1970s and before changed with the birth of recycling. Instead of being seen as a voluntary agreement between debtor nations and creditor institutions on the basis of accepted rules of creditworthiness, borrowing and lending came to be viewed as part of the process of income growth and redistribution, determined by balance of payments considerations. The whole approach to credit assessment changed in ways that were, to a degree, unsound and sustained by a series of fallacies in direct contrast to the simpler and more straightforward rules that had been followed previously.

Sovereign Risk Fallacy

The peculiar characteristic of the lending game after 1973 was that it was no longer possible or practicable for banks to follow the cardinal rule of "know your customer". In some loans, hundreds of banks were involved including all but a few that were merely participants in loan syndications. These banks often had little or no experience in international lending and few, if any, resources to analyse and assess sovereign risk. Even the major banks, with the strength and reputation to negotiate directly with senior debtor government officials, were not in a position to know their clients in the same way that they knew their major corporate customers; nor were their often complex country risk appraisal systems able to provide the vital input into lending decisions which their corporate financial models purported to be able to do. Lending to governments came to be dominated more by the need to finance balance of payments deficits than to finance specific investment projects against which the productivity of the loan could be measured. It is one thing to supplement domestic savings with foreign savings in order to help generate productive assets but quite another to transfer foreign savings to fill the gaps made by excessive consumption or inappropriate economic management.

Banks had no real power over, or in-depth knowledge of, the uses or misuses of the funds which they (willingly) made available. In some cases, debtor governments could not even supply the necessary economic and financial data to support their demands for foreign credit and there were other cases where governments were unable to supply comprehensive and consistent data about the size of their foreign debt, let alone its maturity and currency composition.

The "comfort" that allowed the basic rules of credit to be overlooked was the almost naive belief that sovereign lending was relatively low-risk because countries cannot go bust. We refer to this as the sovereign risk fallacy. The reality was and remains that countries can and do go bust and it is really semantics to argue that they may only fail to honour their external obligations. The only difference between sovereign risk and corporate risk is that when a country cannot meet its obligations, creditors cannot seize and sell the borrower's assets and distribute the proceeds amongst themselves – at least not since the passing of the days of gunboat diplomacy. The fact that debtor governments do own quite substantial real and productive assets is not thought to be relevant because of the political sensitivities of bringing such assets into negotiations with creditors. Politics aside, however, countries do go bust and possess assets which could, in theory, be sold to creditors. The failure to believe that countries could go bust was, at best, a misunderstanding of the concept of sovereign lending and, at worst, an exercise in self-delusion on the part of banks. It is reasonable to ask why banks did not succeed in establishing their country risk creditworthiness criteria more effectively or overlooked them. To answer this we must catch a glimpse of the financial sector's culture of the time. The allocation of bank credit was driven primarily by marketing considerations, i.e. increased revenues based on an ever-expanding volume of loans sold. In part, this was a reaction to the decline in loan spreads that resulted from strong competitive pressures in the international loan market, so that earnings became the key criterion of success – a broken rule, to which we shall return. Aggresive lending to LDCs, however, was also the result of the elevation of marketing considerations over country risk factors. There was an important reason for this development: the country manager or regional head in an international bank was rewarded on the basis of revenues earned and, therefore, of loans sold. In his short-term assignment in a particular country or region he was expected to demonstrate such success as a means of getting promotion to another position, preferably in his home base. Thus, the achievement of narrow, specific, earnings-related financial objectives tended to override the doom and gloom that was the preserve of at least some economic and political analysts.

Even in those institutions where economists were charged with running and forecasting a country risk assessment system, there were no uniform or widespread analytical techniques employed and there was little, if any, assessment of the balance between risk and reward on individual loans. It would hardly be surprising if all country risk systems created a spectrum of risk with Japan and Switzerland at the top and Zaire and Bangladesh on the bottom. Because the pricing of loans was external to and separate from country risk appraisal systems, the profitability of loans was not investigated seriously enough; and because country risk systems dealt in aggregates, ratios and probabilities, there was no way of identifying whether a particular loan to a particular country would be serviced properly or repaid or refinanced without undue pressure. Country risk assessment techniques tended to highlight a family of economic and financial ratios, designed to indicate the probability of a country's likelihood of debt service problems or certain (arbitrary) thresholds which, if surpassed, implied financial distress.

This discipline was fine as far as it went but it was subject to several weaknesses. Firstly, debt statistics were not adequate and it is only since the start of the present decade that the World Bank, IMF, OECD and BIS have begun to make available much more comprehensive and detailed data on foreign debt and even then with still considerable lags. Secondly, statistical risk assessment techniques could not discriminate properly between debtor countries with similar debt ratios; thus, some Latin American countries scored as well, if not better, than some Asian borrowers even up to 1982. The appraisal of country risk in terms of the ratios of debt to GNP, or debt to exports, or even the more popular debt service ratio, did not give enough information or warning about a given country's financial position or ability to service debt. In 1980 (1982 in parenthesis), according to World Bank data, Nigeria had a debt service ratio of 2% (9), the Philippines 7.2% (13.2), Venezuela 13.3% (15.7) and Argentina 17.7% (24.5). All four countries would seek reschedulings within three years. In contrast, Pakistan had a debt service ratio of 11.1% (9.3), South Korea 12% (13.1), Egypt 15.4% (30.7), and Algeria 24.9% (27.2) and none has had recourse to creditors to alter the terms of their debt. Thirdly, country risk assessment warnings were often overridden or diluted by other factors in the lending decision-making process.

To summarise the sovereign risk fallacy, *the state of the art of*

*country risk appraisal was not an adequate substitute for the risk
assessment techniques which young commercial bankers learned on
the job in their dealings with local companies.* Without adequate
risk assessment techniques and with a sort of lending bias that
resulted from internal pressures within banks and the banking
industry, loans were "protected" only by the belief that sovereign
governments could always pay their debts.

The sovereign risk fallacy comes full circle

Unfortunately for banks, the sovereign risk fallacy was accentuated by banking practices which were also a significant departure
from basic principles. At the same time as international loan
spreads were being reduced owing to substantial competitive
pressures, banks engaged in a major effort to increase their
business volume, i.e. to market their loans aggressively (involving
substantial increases in the fixed costs associated with such a
strategy), so as to be able to continue paying attractive dividends to
shareholders and maintain the share prices of their institutions. In
effect, therefore, banks were paying out to shareholders the capital
they ought to have been setting aside and accumulating while
growing their low-spread, small-return assets rapidly. The result,
of course, was the tendency for capital adequacy (ratio of capital to
assets) to decline below prudent levels.

When the crisis broke during and after 1982, banks were faced
with the full implications of their practices over the previous
decade. They were heavily exposed as regards bad debts concentrated in several major borrower nations and representing a
multiple of their capital. As a result, they were obliged to make
large loan loss reserves, which are a charge against earnings but
may not be treated as capital. Financial markets, having recognised
the seriousness of the decline in the financial health of commercial
banks, traded bank shares down to between 35% and 65% (in the
case of US banks) of their book value. Banks were therefore unable
to build up their capital sufficiently through either retained
earnings or share issues and could only raise their capital to asset
ratios by shrinking the size of their assets and improving the
profitability of those assets, i.e. slow down sharply (or reduce) the
growth of assets, eliminate some borrowers from the portfolio and
charge higher spreads. As banks continue to go through this
adjustment – of restoring capital adequacy, slowing down interna-

tional loan growth and pricing and allocating loans to take better account of risk – the more traditional rules of international lending are being readopted and applied – at least for the time being.

The oil-in-the-ground fallacy

The oil shocks in the 1970s gave rise to the belief that oil-producing countries, especially those that were, or would rapidly become, net oil exporters, were particularly attractive countries to which to lend. This belief was based on the substantial increase in wealth that accrued to such countries and on the expectation that oil prices would continue to rise as sharply, if not more so, in the next decade or so, as had been the case in the 1970s. Thus, although OPEC countries with small populations were either net suppliers of funds or had only a limited demand for credit, other OPEC countries such as Venezuela and Nigeria and non-OPEC oil producers such as Mexico, Bolivia, Egypt, Tunisia and Malaysia were seen as good risks.

The fallacy was extended to countries with other non-oil natural resources, such as Poland with its substantial coal reserves. As with oil, however, the belief rested on the assumption that commodity prices, especially energy, would continue to rise in real terms, i.e. faster than world inflation. The collapse of prices after 1981 hit all commodity-based debtor countries and undermined economic development projects that were financed and started in a radically different economic environment – a subject we shall come back to shortly.

The umbrella fallacy

The umbrella fallacy was the rule that indicated that lending to some countries was relatively risk-free if those countries fell within or beneath the political umbrella of either the USA or the USSR. The basis for this belief was the economic and financial support made available to satellite countries or those with particular vital economic or military significance. Before the overthrow of the Shah of Iran, this vital Middle-East oil-producing nation was thought to have the protection of the USA which, in the end, it was unable to offer in any form. The umbrella was full of holes and the USA was unable to arrest the drift into financial chaos. Eastern Europe was deemed to have a sort of unwritten guarantee from the

USSR and banks increased their exposure in the region and to the USSR itself. This involvement developed during the period of détente between the major powers and commercial interests on both sides were encouraged by this process. The umbrella was, however, full of holes. In 1980, political unrest in Poland contributed to a severe deterioration in the country's economic situation, resulting in its inability to meet its debt-service obligations without across-the-board and, as it turned out, continuous rescheduling. There was no USSR bail-out and the banks reacted by adopting more restrictive policies with respect to other eastern European countries whose underlying economic situation was in part quite different. New credits to eastern European countries, which had expanded to $6.8 billion in 1980, slowed down to $4.7 billion in 1981 and there were actual credit withdrawals of $4.7 billion in 1982. The principal victim of this "regionalization syndrome" was Hungary which, unlike other eastern European countries, had been financing the bulk of its foreign trade in the Euro-market and had, therefore, run up very substantial debts to the banks – a significant proportion of them short-term. Despite the fact that the authorities had embarked on an adjustment programme in 1979 which by 1981 had turned the foreign trade account from deficit to surplus, increased interest payments produced a marked deterioration of the current-account balance, compounded by very large withdrawals of short-term banking funds in the first quarter of 1982. In order to stabilize the situation, emergency credits were granted by the BIS to the National Bank of Hungary; and this was followed by further domestic adjustment measures and an IMF credit with the result that Hungary was eventually able to obtain some new financial accommodation from the banks.

Indeed, the debt crisis that struck most of the Latin American continent was partly caused by the reaction of creditors and investors to the official US support given to the UK during the Falkland Islands war with Argentina in May 1982. The US Administration's aid and support to the UK was interpreted unfavourably insofar as loans and investments made in a Latin America with full US backing were seen as more stable and secure than a Latin America without it. Although Argentina stressed its willingness to stand by its financial obligations, the Falklands war did, of course, have consequences for its debt-servicing capacity. Moreover, by heightening the banks' awareness of their risk exposure in Latin America generally, it prepared the way for a "regionalization syndrome" in that part of the world too, so that other Latin American countries saw their access to international bank credit becoming more difficult and more expensive. The Falklands conflict highlighted the fact that American banks had an exposure in Latin America well beyond their capital and reserves, an exposure that could be viewed as prudent only if there was an expectation that the US would come to the aid of these countries in the event that the region fell into a serious payments crisis. The decision by the US to support Britain rather than Argentina in the South Atlantic conflict exploded the credibility of that assumption and unnerved bankers, causing the flow of funds to Latin America to decline drastically.

Though the Falklands factor alone would not have caused the Latin American debt crisis, it was certainly a contributory factor when economic fears for the region were already mounting. In a number of countries that have had to reschedule their foreign debt, bank lending – especially short-term lending – began to slow down or decline around six months before the debt crisis actually erupted and there can be little doubt that political fears and uncertainty, arising from another fallacy, were instrumental.

Short-term lending fallacy

In the basic principles of lending, it was suggested that one key convention was not to borrow short and lend long. For if short-term (funding) interest rates rose above long-term (lending) interest rates, the lender would suffer a loss. Furthermore, short-term deposits could be withdrawn quite quickly and the bank could be faced with a severe liquidity and/or solvency crisis. However, the advent of floating-rate financial instruments meant that, so long as banks could continue to sell loans at reasonable spreads, any rise in the bank's borrowing costs could be passed on to the recipient of the loan. The belief that international lending could continue on this basis, we refer to as the short-term lending fallacy.

As countries faced increasing debt-service charges and their reserves began to decline, the demand for short-term credit rose sharply. At the same time banks, already acting more warily, felt more exposed in making long-term loans than by keeping loan maturities short. In the event, the expansion of short-term lending (see Table 5.7) was the Achilles' Heel for both banks and countries. The greater and the more rapid was the accumulation of short-term debt, the bigger was the debt-service burden and a vicious circle was formed. Thus, when confidence in such countries as Mexico, Brazil and Hungary began to fade, short-term bank credit which had already been growing more slowly, was promptly withdrawn (though in Mexico's case, this was short-lived).

Table 5.7. Short-Term Assets* and Undisbursed
Credit Commitments of BIS Banks (% Assets)

	Mid-1978	*End-1982*	*End-1983*
To: Eastern Europe	55.9	45.8	47.1
All LDCs	59.0	56.1	54.5
Latin America	52.7	50.3	47.5
Middle East	76.4	83.2	83.3
Africa	49.1	44.9	43.3
Asia	66.2	61.8	60.2

* *Assets with a maturity up to and including one year.*

Source: BIS

The austerity fallacy

One of the more recent fallacies is that major debtors can regain some financial strength if they undergo a period of austerity. The basis of the co-operation between commercial banks and the IMF, is the rescheduling arrangements between debtor and creditor governments and of the provision of new bank money to rescheduling countries in agreement with the IMF adjustment programme, which is designed to restore external balance through reducing demand and barriers to supply. However, austerity is also likely to become a self-defeating strategy the more generalised it becomes. A sharp decline in domestic demand and in imports in one country hits the export revenues of other countries with which it trades and which are, themselves, attempting to reduce imports. A general contraction in trade and income ensues, therefore, and creates pressure for further austerity measures in the absence of new credit inflows and particularly when debtor countries are paying more in debt-service obligations than they are receiving in new loans. Such a situation is clearly unstable and unsustainable and will lead eventually to stronger deflationary forces in world economic activity. The focus needs to change towards economic growth and the expansion of exports as the panacea for problems of chronic indebtedness accompanied, of course, by more conservative domestic economic management, where appropriate. For the social and political fall-out of continuing austerity, lack of growth and falling living standards, could undermine much more than the financial relationships between debtor governments and creditor institutions.

The irony of the austerity fallacy is that once debtors have agreed to implement austerity programmes, they do qualify for IMF funds and banks will reschedule their debts, extend the debt maturity profile and make some limited new finance available. Debtor countries pay fees to banks to obtain these concessions and new finance tends to be absorbed by the payment of fees and debt-servicing on existing debt. Banks record these payments as income but they are only the equivalent of the new money they have lent. Thus, foreign debt continues to increase, debt service peaks are pushed out three to four years and banks and debtor governments hope that, in the meantime, the financial position will improve as commodity prices recover and interest rates decline. The pursuit of austerity programmes and the global deflationary impulses which they generate may indeed be consistent with the prospect for lower interest rates but not with higher commodity prices. Similarly and conversely, the conditions which support higher commodity prices are unlikely to be consistent with the prospects for lower interest rates.

Capital adequacy and LDC lending

In Chapter 1, we discussed some issues relating to the concept of bank capital and observed both the decline in capital ratios and, in the case of the USA, recent regulatory initiatives. Here we look again at bank capital in the specific context of LDC lending.

At the middle of 1983, the capital-asset ratio of all BIS banks (see Table 5.8) with regard to thirteen major LDC borrowers stood at 76.9%. As regards all LDCs, including Eastern Europe, the ratio stood at 115.2%. As is shown below, over one third of banks' capital is at risk from just two countries, Mexico and Brazil.

Table 5.8. Distribution of BIS Banks' Claims ($billion)
and in Relation to Capital* (% in Parenthesis)

Argentina	25.5 (6.9)	Indonesia	10.9 (2.9)	Nigeria	9.2 (2.5)
Brazil	62.8 (17.0)	S. Korea	22.7 (6.1)	Poland	12.2 (3.3)
Chile	10.9 (2.9)	Malaysia	7.9 (2.1)	Yugoslavia	9.6 (2.6)
Mexico	65.5 (17.7)	Philippines	13.3 (3.6)		
Venezuela	26.8 (7.2)	Algeria	7.1 (1.9)		
	Total of Above:		284.4 (76.9)		
	Total of all LDCs:		426.4 (115.2)		

(* Estimated at $335 billion at end 1981 (IMF) and assumed to have grown by 5% per year in 1982-1983.)

Source: BIS

Table 5.9. US Banks' Capital Ratios

All US Banks	1977	1978	1979	1980	1981	1982
Eastern Europe	16.7	15.8	16.1	13.9	12.9	8.2
Non-oil LDC's	114.9	114.4	124.2	132.2	148.3	146.1
Total	131.6	130.2	140.3	146.2	163.5	155.0
(Mexico	27.4	23.4	23.0	27.6	34.3	34.5)
Nine Largest US Banks						
Eastern Europe	25.0	23.5	23.9	21.8	19.5	13.9
Non-oil LDC's	163.2	166.8	82.1	199.3	220.6	221.2
Total	188.2	190.3	206.0	221.1	240.1	235.2
(Mexico	32.9	30.4	29.6	37.8	44.4	44.4)
(Brazil	41.9	42.4	40.3	39.3	40.8	45.8)

Nine Largest Banks (1982)	Argentina	Brazil	Mexico	Venezuela	Chile	Total of 5
Citicorp	18.2	73.5	54.6	18.2	10.0	174.5
Bank of America	10.2	47.9	52.1	41.7	6.3	158.2
Chase Manhattan	21.3	56.9	40.0	24.0	11.8	154.0
Manufacturers' Hanover	47.5	77.7	66.7	42.4	28.4	262.4
J.P. Morgan	24.4	54.3	34.8	17.5	9.7	140.7
Chemical	14.9	52.0	60.0	8.0	14.8	169.7
Continental Illinois	17.8	22.9	32.4	21.6	12.8	107.5
First Interstate	6.9	43.9	63.0	18.5	3.7	136.0
Bankers Trust	13.2	46.2	46.2	25.1	10.6	141.2

Source: William R. Cline, *International Debt and Stability of the World Economy* (1983)

Although most national banking groups have a high exposure to Latin America, US banks have by far the largest share of total lending to countries in the region and it is they who have most at risk in terms of assets outstanding, geographic concentration and capital adequacy. Table 5.9 shows the aggregate capital-asset ratios for all US banks, for the nine largest US banks and then for some individual banks in relation to a small group of borrowers.

By the end of 1983, these capital ratios had improved slightly because banks had started to slow down their asset growth and build up some capital. However, interesting developments occurred within the US banking sector. US regional banks, which had been attracted to LDC lending in the 1970s cut their relative exposure to four major Latin American borrowers three times as much as did the biggest nine US banks, thereby shifting the risk concentration more towards the biggest banks (see Table 5.10).

Table 5.10. US Bank Lending to four Major Latin Borrowers (End 1983 $billion)

	Largest 9 Banks	Next Largest 15 Banks	185 other Banks	Total
Mexico	14.1	5.3	6.9	26.3
Brazil	13.3	4.3	3.1	20.7
Venezuela	7.6	2.1	1.5	11.3
Argentina	5.4	2.0	1.2	8.5
Total Loans	40.4	13.7	12.7	66.8
Capital	31.5	14.9	33.0	79.4
Total Loans/Capital (%)	128.3	91.9	38.5	84.1
Memo: Change in Loans Since June 1982:	+2.6	+1.5	−0.6	+3.5

Source: *Federal Financial Institutions Examination Council (1984)*

The regional banks managed in 1983 to reduce their loans outstanding by $600 million and cut their exposure from 50.4 to 38.5% of capital. The biggest banks had to increase their loans by just over $2.5 billion and could only improve their capital ratio from 139.4 to 128.3%.

Confidence and stability in banking depends, in the first instance, on the behaviour and actions of individual banks and the ways in which they manage the risks involved in funding (taking deposits) and in making loans. Banks have a variety of internal systems to measure and control credit evaluation and credit limits but the most important safeguard of all is the maintenance of sufficient capital so that losses can be absorbed without running the risk of being declared insolvent. The management problem for banks is that the larger the capital the better the ability to absorb losses; but the larger (in relation to assets) is the capital the lower will be potential profitability.

Whilst lower capital ratios for bigger banks may be justified on the grounds that they have larger scope for diversifying assets and may therefore bear less risk of major losses than smaller banks, it is clear that the capital position of even the largest banks has become threatened. The geographic concentration of loans in banks' portfolios and the difficulties in raising equity capital (because of investors' concerns about the vulnerability of banks) have simply made capital appear inadequate to cover the losses that might be incurred if only a few countries defaulted on, or repudiated, their debt.

Recent regulatory initiatives

In the USA banks have set aside the least in terms of reserves against loan losses. However, the regulatory authorities are tightening the standards applied to loan loss provisions. In November 1983, in return for agreeing to increase the US contribution to the IMF, Congress insisted that the Federal Reserve lay down more restrictive provisions, as discussed in Chapter 1. As a result, banks had to make provisions of between 10 and 50% against loans to so-called "value-impaired" countries. However, in general, banks have made fewer sovereign provisions than European banks, partly because of relatively unfavourable tax treatment in the US where sovereign debt provisions are considered to be part of general provisions, i.e. against risks that are not yet specific or identified they are not usually offsettable against tax.

In the UK banks have made large but undisclosed bad-debt provisions under the aegis of the Bank of England, while in West Germany, the Federal Banking Supervisory Office has unofficially urged banks to step up their provisions against bad debts, including a minimum 40% against loans to Poland. The Japanese Ministry of Finance has insisted that banks provide from 1.5 to 5% of loans made to a list of thirty-three countries which have delayed making debt payments or rescheduled and the Swiss Federal

Banking Commission has instructued all banks to set aside a minimum 20% of the value of their problem loans to debtor countries. French banks are thought to have set aside some 20% of their Latin American loans but, since the bulk of the French banking system is nationalized, it is arguable that the taxpayer is an ultimate and automatic lender-of-last-resort to any bank that encountered serious problems.

By and large, it appears that major continental European banks made rather larger country risk provision against a wider range of countries than did banks headquartered in other countries. This has been attributable, probably, to improved earnings performance, strong supervisory encouragement and the favourable tax treatment of specific provisions.

There seems little doubt that banks worldwide will continue, for the foreseeable future, to try to build up their capital. In the US Federal regulations or guidelines are likely to require banks to meet higher capital ratios. In Europe, where banks did not experience the same rate of decline in their ratios or where banking systems may already be largely nationalized, the need to restore capital is not as urgent but it is just as necessary.

Any bank that has to make special reserves or provisions against increased LDC risk out of capital or retained earnings will experience slower growth of capital or the need to reduce dividends or both and either will depress the bank's share price. The relative weakness of bank share prices in 1984 meant that banks have had to resort to other forms of capital-raising but, more importantly, to resort to cutting back the growth of assets – particularly the less profitable and riskier ones.

Assessment of the role of banks

The major fact for banks in their international lending activities is that their role as the dominant financial intermediaries between OPEC countries and non-oil LDCs has declined. The major question is whether banks will be able and willing to continue lending on the scale required to help the process of orderly economic adjustment in LDCs.

Having effectively recycled the OPEC surplus again in 1979-1980, banks were confronted after 1981 with continuing large credit demands from non-oil LDCs, growing credit demands from OPEC and a large withdrawal of deposits by OPEC countries ($32

Table 5.11. The End of Recycling ($billion)

	1978	1979	1980	1981	1982	1983	1984
Net Deposits from OPEC	−13.5	30.2	34.9	−1.0	−26.4	−23.1	3.7
Net Borrowing by non-oil LDCs	−8.2	−23.0	−35.1	−30.5	−14.9	−1.6	13.0
Banks Total Net Lending	−21.7	7.2	−0.2	−31.5	−41.3	−24.7	16.7

Source: BIS

billion in 1982-1983). The net lending to these groups of nations peaked at over $41 billion in 1982 and had it not been for the build-up in LDC reserves and bank deposits, the financing strains would have been even bigger. The incidence of widespread and large debt reschedulings, the need to continue growing exposure in a few debtor countries and the perceived inadequacy of capital, have changed radically lenders' perception of risk and so set in motion a sharp deceleration in the volume of new international lending, culminating in 1984 in net deposits of nearly $17 billion (Table 5.11).

In the future, the banks' role in financing LDCs will be much reduced. Even if LDCs' credit demands slow down as a result of austerity, IMF programmes and slower economic growth, the real issue is whether banks will be *able* to provide the financing (since amounts involved will remain large in terms of asset growth) and whether banks will be *willing* to provide the financing. The pressures to protect and build capital, re-allocate some LDC risk to smaller or less mature industrial countries and avoid (at least) further increases in LDC exposure, imply a much more defensive attitude on the part of the banks. The fall-out is likely to include a sharp drop in the number of banks involved in international lending, a return to higher lending spreads for several countries and a sustained decline in the rate of growth in the international interbank market partly because of balance-sheet-inflation and the low-return nature of such business.

Banks generally are now more co-operative and act more collectively than in the 1970s when aggresive, asset-driven strategies lead to a proliferation of banks, low returns and an undesirable growth in exposure and concentration. Today, the need to agree debt-rescheduling terms may involve hundreds of banks and the ability to protect existing assets involves co-operation with the IMF – however "involuntary" such co-operation might be.

The role of banks in the debt game has changed as the stakes have become too big and the threat of loss too real. The banks are no longer in a position to control the outcome of the game which has ceased to have a purely economic character and which will become increasingly political where power and leverage are the goals. In the end someone somewhere has to pay the price for the loans to LDCs that turned out to be excessive and of poor risk. Borrower nations have been paying for it in terms of declining living standards and slower growth. Creditor governments are going to have to pay for it in terms of increased taxation, whether for the IMF or to bail out failed banks. Banks are going to pay for it through writing off loans and strains on earnings and profits. The outcome of the power and leverage tussle will determine who pays what proportion of the price. As things stand, the bank shareholder and the taxpayer seem likely to have to bear the brunt of the money costs, if the debt crisis should continue to deteriorate. The social and political costs in debtor countries, however, will be – and in some countries, for example, in Africa, are – far more pervasive and in human terms, incalculable.

Chapter 6
The Role of
Governments

The second major group of players in the debt game are the governments of both industrial countries (creditor governments) and of LDCs (debtor governments). The relationship between the two has always been an obviously political one, whose outcome depends on the leverage that derives from economic power. In this chapter, we shall consider the debt game from the perspective of both debtor and creditor governments. As creditor governments have become more and more involved in the debt situation, in contrast to the 1970s, the political nature of the situation has become increasingly apparent. The behaviour of debtor governments is vital also because any move to repudiate debt or withdraw from the international financial system is first and foremost a political act.

DEBTOR GOVERNMENTS
Types of debtor

In discussing the debt crisis and debtor governments, it is important to distinguish between the types of debtor countries in the international financial system.

The first group comprises a few advanced LDCs which have relatively diversified economies and which are significant exporters of manufactured products. These countries are mostly in Latin America and South East Asia, for example, Argentina, Brazil, Hong Kong, Korea and Singapore but include such countries as Greece and Israel. They owe most of their long-term debt to private creditors (around 69% in 1984), the majority of which is to banks and the proportion of their short-term debt (which fell from 23% in 1982 to around 15% in 1984 largely because of rescheduling) is higher than for all non-OPEC LDCs.

The bulk of their debt is on floating-rate terms and they are, therefore, vulnerable to sharp fluctuations in market interest rates. By and large, though, the debt burden for Latin America is much heavier than that for Asian countries.

The second group of debtors is the net oil-exporting nations, which do not belong to OPEC. These countries also owe a high proportion of their long-term debt to private creditors (over 60%) and also mostly on floating rate terms. Nearly 45% of their long-term debt is owed to banks. Short-term debt accounted for about 12% of total debt, down from over 24% in 1982. Such countries include, Bolivia, Congo, Egypt, Malaysia, Mexico, Peru, Syria and Tunisia.

In the same group are other, mostly middle-income non-oil producing LDCs, which owe around 45 to 46% of their long-term debt to private creditors but only 29% to banks. Official creditors account for nearly 40% of long-term debt.

The third group comprises forty-three countries whose per capita GDP is the lowest in the world. These are the poorest, commodity-dependent nations, mostly in Africa, which rely mostly on official development assistance and officially extended or guaranteed export credits. Around 83% of long-term debt is owed to official creditors, while only 15% is owed to banks. The proportion of short-term debt fell from over 6% in 1979 to 2 to 3% in 1983-1984.

Finally, there are the countries in Eastern Europe, the USSR and other socialist economies, which receive no aid from the IMF and World Bank (except for Hungary and Yugoslavia which are members) but which have received credits from Western governments on a bilateral basis and from banks.

It is useful to recall that some, mostly Asian debtor countries, have survived the debt crisis rather better than most other countries. It is no accident that the bulk of the world's debt problems are concentrated in Latin America and, to a lesser extent, parts of Eastern Europe and Africa. So far as Latin America is concerned, economic development strategies have reflected a totally different range of priorities from those pursued in Asia. For at least a decade before the 1970s, Latin American countries had tried to restrict the growth of imports by recourse to tariffs and quotas, to the substitution of subsidized domestic production for imports and by subsidized promotion of the export of manufactured goods. Such policies as we discussed in chapter 5 may frequently be associated with inefficiency, because they penalise the use of low-cost substitutes and encourage resources to be misused or misallocated. These nations also had large state bureaucracies, which held substantial stakes in productive enterprises and concentrated planning and decision-making power as regards prices, subsidies and exchange rate management.

These forms of economic management may be compared with the more flexible, market- and export-oriented economic strategies adopted by Hong Kong, Singapore and Malaysia, which also tended to be more accomodative towards foreign investment and private sector economic activity. All LDCs were, of course, vulnerable to, and seriously affected by, the rise in interest rates that occurred after 1980 but it is clear that Asian borrowers had an underlying strength which was found lacking in Latin America and also in the relatively more backward economies in Africa and the state-run economies of Eastern Europe. (It is no accident that Hungary's economic "success", relatively speaking, owes much to that country's relatively liberal economic policies as regards initiative and reward.) These economies were already more vulnerable to external shocks and, therefore, less capable of being managed to overcome them.

To the extent that governments pursued economic development strategies that fostered the spread of inefficiency, inflexibility and low productivity, it might be argued that their foreign borrowing was unsound and mismanaged. We shall look at the subject of mistakes and mismanagement later in this chapter.

Why governments borrow abroad

In recent times, it has become common to look upon the major debtor countries as all being profligate spenders or to see foreign borrowing as an unnecessary luxury or bad policy. However, foreign borrowing provides important benefits to countries and all those that embark on economic development need to borrow abroad since they lack domestic capital, both physical and human.

Because they have immature and underdeveloped capital markets and institutions, developing economies must attract foreign savings to make up for the shortage of domestic savings in order to finance capital investment programmes, the development of local industry and to relieve the shortage of foreign exchange. Foreign borrowing allows a country to develop economically and overcome these two critical shortfalls, savings and foreign exchange.

The underlying reason why countries borrow and lend can be couched in terms of supply and demand: if, at prevailing world interest rates a country's demand for investible funds exceeds the supply generated within its borders, residents of the country may borrow the difference from foreign lenders; or, if a country's demand for investible funds falls short of the supply generated within its borders, the excess supply may be loaned to foreign borrowers. Thus shifts in a country's demand or supply of investible funds can produce changes in the country's international borrowing or lending.

What is responsible for shifts in a country's supply of or demand for investible funds? In real terms, the supply of investible funds is derived from saving which, at any given interest rate, depends largely upon the income of the savers and their time preference, i.e., how they choose to allocate their income over time between present and future consumption. The demand for investible funds, on the other hand, depends essentially upon the return expected to be earned from investment. Consequently, shifts in the income or time preference of savers, or shifts in the expected returns available from investment, can bring about changes in international lending at any given interest rate.

It follows that net lending or borrowing does not signify a maladjustment or a disequilibrium. On the contrary, if a block of savings in a country will not yield as high a return in that country as in another country, a loan from the first to the second country will generally be in the interests of both; on a global scale, world income and trade will be higher then than if countries had remained closed and autarchic.

A less developed country may, therefore, borrow abroad for two main purposes. Firstly, borrowing allows the country to finance investment and infrastructure projects which will increase future output, exports, and income. Over time, the accumulation of foreign exchange should permit the country to slow down the growth of foreign debt to the point where net repayments of debt begin to take place. Eventually, in theory, economic development will reach the stage at which the country's availability of savings allow it to start lending abroad and to grow into a net creditor nation. Secondly, foreign borrowing may be a convenient and effective way of spreading the costs of economic adjustment over a long period or to buy time within which to sort out temporary economic disturbances. Examples of the latter include crop failures, natural disasters, and a cyclical downturn in major export markets, while the former refers more to the modernization of agriculture or build-up of new or more advanced industries.

How much should a country borrow?

The amount of debt to contract is a basic policy decision, and the correct decision will depend on the skill and judgement of those responsible for making it. Formal models and related technical analyses cannot substitute for good policymaking, but they can aid by providing information on the future implications of alternative borrowing strategies – especially their impact on a country's capacity to invest wisely in the light of its balance of payments prospects.

The amount that any country ought to borrow is governed by two factors: firstly, how much foreign capital the economy can absorb efficiently and secondly, how much debt it can service without risking external payment problems.

Each factor will depend on the effectiveness of overall economic management but, considered narrowly, after the debt-servicing capacity of the economy is projected, the volume of external borrowing will depend on the terms on which it is made available. Most governments, in assessing the feasibility of a borrowing strategy, pay particular attention to the risk of overtaking their debt-servicing capacity and causing balance of payments problems but they also examine the costs, in terms of foregone growth, of underborrowing. In foreign borrowing both over-optimism and excessive pessimism can be costly.

A country's borrowing should not unduly mortgage the country's future. This condition is fulfilled so long as: firstly, the funds obtained are used to increase investment; secondly, the investment benefits export and/or import-substitution industries sufficiently to allow the resulting external debt to be serviced without a drastic deterioration in the country's terms of trade and thirdly, the productivity of the investment is, taking into account the second factor delineated above, commensurate with its real interest cost.

So when a country borrows for temporary or short-term economic adjustment purposes, it must be assumed that the borrower (and the lender) know that the situation is temporary and reversible. The amount of borrowing might be determined on the basis of similar situations or the worst situation in the past. In the case of development financing, the rate of return on the projects to be financed is the critical measure. Debt can grow without limit provided that the rate of return is higher than the cost of servicing the debt – a proviso that all the players in the game overlooked in the 1970's and early 1980's.

To illustrate the above point more specifically, a country's stock of debt can grow faster than output (a rise in the ratio of Debt to GDP) only if the real rate of interest is less than the rate of growth of output. Otherwise, the increase in output will be exhausted by the higher real interest rate and there will be no income with which to service the debt; as we have observed and shall see later the rise in real interest rates and collapse of economic growth in debtor countries dealt a devastating blow to the financial viability of many LDCs.

Moreover, it should be self-evident that foreign borrowing to pay for debt-servicing or for growing domestic budget deficits or for oil imports cannot be sustained in the absence of radical economic reforms designed to generate higher export revenues, tax revenues or energy savings. The fact that many LDCs could not or did not undertake such reforms when the global economic environment comprised low real interest rates and high economic growth meant that they faced particularly severe problems when real interest rates soared and economic activity became stagnant.

Modelling of the behaviour of sovereign borrowers and private creditors?

In the textbook model of the loan market borrowers have ready access to loans at a given interest rate; they enter the loan market to finance all investment projects with a positive present value at the prevailing interest rate and they use loans to equate the marginal utility of consumption at different points in time. If demand for loans should exceed supply, interest rates will rise, decreasing demand and/or increasing supply until demand and supply are equated at the new equilibrium interest rate.

Actual lending behaviour is not like this. Borrowers may face extensive rationing in the international markets. They may be unable to obtain credit at any price, much less the posted market price. Highly profitable investment projects may be left standing for want of foreign capital, or worse, may be abandoned mid-stream after creditors withdraw capital in a sudden loss of confidence.

Stiglitz and Weiss[1] have convincingly argued that in equilibrium a loan market may be characterized by credit-rationing. That is, given an excess demand for funds, rather than raise the rate of interest banks ration the available supply of funds among their borrowers according to such criteria as the borrower's credit rating, the amount of business he does, *etc*. The reason for this is that banks, in making loans, are concerned about the interest rate they receive on the loan and the riskiness of the loan. However, the interest rate a bank charges may itself affect the riskiness of the pool of loans by either sorting potential borrowers (the adverse selection effect); or affecting the actions of borrowers (the incentive effect).

Both effects derive directly from the residual imperfect information which is present in loan markets after banks have evaluated loan applications. When the price (interest rate) affects the nature of the transaction, it may not also clear the market.

The adverse selection aspect of interest rates is a consequence of different borrowers having different probabilities of repaying their loan. The expected return to the bank obviously depends on the probability of repayment, so the bank would like to be able to identify borrowers who are more likely to repay. It is difficult to identify "good borrowers" and to do so requires the bank to use a variety of screening devices. The interest rate which an individual is willing to pay may act as one such screening device: those who are willing to pay high interest rates may, on average, be worse risks – they are willing to borrow at high interest rates because they perceive their probability of repaying the loan to be low. As the interest rate rises, the average "riskiness" of those who borrow

[1] J. Stiglitz and A. Weiss, "Credit Rationing in Markets with Imperfect Information", *American Economic Review* (June 1981).

increases, possibly lowering the bank's profits. Similarly, as the interest rate and other terms of the contract change, the behaviour of the borrower is likely to change. For instance, raising the interest rate decreases the return on projects which succeed. We will show that higher interest rates induce firms to undertake projects with lower probabilities of success but higher payoffs when successful.

In a world with perfect and costless information the bank would stipulate precisely all the actions which the borrower could undertake (which might affect the return to the loan). However, the bank is not able to control directly all the actions of the borrower therefore it will formulate the terms of the loan contract in a manner designed to induce the borrower to take actions which are in the interest of the bank, as well as to attract low-risk borrowers.

For both these reasons the expected return by the bank may increase less rapidly than the interest rate and, beyond a point, may actually decrease.

Stiglitz and Weiss illustrate that credit rationing can occur when lenders cannot evaluate the risk categories of possible borrowers. Eaton and Gersovitz[2] specified and tested an economic model of borrowing by poor countries in international financial markets. They stressed the view that unless the governments of private creditors were willing to coerce lender governments into repaying loans there is no explicit mechanism detering them from repudiating external debt. However, even without legal or coercive methods of enforcing repayment, private creditors can take a number of retaliatory actions to penalize defaulting debtors. Among the most important of these penalties is exclusion from future borrowing.

Working with the assumption that this exclusion is permanent, they were able to show that lenders will establish a credit above which they will be unwilling to increase loans. The amount of this ceiling is determined by lenders' perception of borrowers' disutility of exclusion. If the ceiling is below the amount a borrower wishes to obtain then the borrower is rationed. Their theoretical model relates both the credit ceiling and the demand for credit to a set of observable borrower characteristics. Using this theoretical

[2] J. Eaton and M. Gersovitz, "Debt with Potential Repudiation", *Review of Economic Studies* (April 1981).

framework as a guide, they specified and estimated the relation
between loan demand and supply and a set of country characteristics. The empirical results coincided quite closely with the
structure of their theory. So Eaton and Gersovitz illustrated how
the presence of sovereign risk could explain credit rationing.

As Sachs[3] has shown the key to modelling debt repudiation is to
measure the benefits and the costs of so doing. The benefits are
straightforward: the borrower saves the real value of the outstanding debt, which is no longer serviced. The costs are far more
problematical. One aspect of the cost is a partial or complete
inability to obtain new loans in the world capital markets, at least
for some time after the repudiation occurs. Another aspect of the
cost may be a direct seizure of the country's overseas assets
including bank accounts, direct foreign investments, ships and
aircraft. A third cost may be a dramatic decline in the country's
capacity to engage in trade. Any form of trade credit following a
repudiation would be difficult to arrange. Sachs in turn found that
credit rationing did occur with the amount of the bank lending
being based on borrowers' reactions to the above penalties of
default.

Mistakes and mismanagement

We have discussed some of the key criteria that should have guided
foreign borrowing but were overlooked or overridden and we have
cited some of the external environmental circumstances which
caused or aggravated serious economic problems in LDCs. The oil
price rises of the 1970s constitute the archetypal example. The
oil-price-induced current-account deficits, unavoidable as they
were, meant that much borrowing did not have a domestic
investment counterpart but was merely additional balance of
payment financing. Moreover, much of the borrowing that was
done at or near zero real interest rates would have appeared
unsound if the more recent levels of interest rates had been
foreseen. And even to the extent that investments were directed to
building up the borrowing countries' export potential, the present
weakness of world demand and the spreading protectionist
tendencies in the industrial countries mean that for the time being
some of these investments cannot bear fruit. Thus, with the benefit
of the hindsight provided by the present world economic situation,
it is not easy to escape the conclusion that international borrowing

[3] J. Sachs, "Theoretical Issues in International Borrowing", NBFR Working
Paper, No. 1189 (Aug. 1983).

since 1974 has not always been very advantageous to the debtor countries, although a good part of it was an inevitable product of the oil price increases.

Evidence concerning the appropriateness of the acquisition of foreign debt is rather ambiguous. Economic growth rates declined by far less in the 1970s *vis-à-vis* the 1960s compared with industrial countries (see Table 6.1), despite the currency problems that followed the breakdown of the Bretton Woods monetary system in 1971 and the oil shocks in 1973 and 1979.

Table 6.1. Economic Growth (Real GDP, %)

	1960-1970	1970-1980	70s as % 60s
All LDCs	5.8	5.6	97
Sub-Sahara Africa	4.7	3.7	79
East Asia & Pacific	7.3	6.9	95
Latin America	5.5	5.5	100
N. Africa & M. East	7.7	8.1	105
Industrial Countries	5.1	3.3	65

Source: World Bank

The maintenance of growth rates in the 1970s was principally permitted by a sharp deterioration in the balance of payments performance of the LDCs but there is evidence that foreign financing of the external deficits was, in part, designed to support capital spending rather than consumption. Since the terms of trade for LDCs (relationship of export prices to import prices) deteriorated in the 1970s, the maintenance of investment/GDP ratios implies that some borrowers must have succeeded in matching increased foreign debt with increased domestic assets (see Table 6.2).

Table 6.2. Investment/GNP Ratios (%)

	1973-1977	1978-1982
Brazil	23.6	21.3
Korea	25.2	31.0
Philippines	21.4	25.6
Taiwan	27.8	28.3
Morocco	22.0	22.8
Algeria	43.0	38.8
Indonesia	20.0	22.0
Mexico	20.8	24.5
Venezuela	28.4	29.4
Nigeria	23.8	25.6

Source: IMF

Although it cannot be said without qualification that borrowers abused the funds they borrowed in the 1970s, it is true that at least part of their external borrowings were channelled into paying for higher-priced oil imports and it is also true that some countries experienced large outflows of capital which foreign borrowing financed to a greater or lesser degree. Furthermore, it is indisputable that economic policies and economic management in many debtor nations were inappropriate to the extent that increased foreign borrowing occurred alongside, for example, widening budget deficits and overvalued currencies.

As discussed above, pride of place in explaining the debt crisis is often given to the oil price explosion of the 1970s. As Meltzer[4] has illustrated, however, this explanation while not entirely wrong, is far from being entirely correct. The principal debtors include Mexico – an oil exporter, Argentina – a country close to energy self-sufficiency and Brazil – a large importer of oil. The problem debtors also include several large countries of Eastern Europe notably Poland, Romania and Yugoslavia. One is an oil-producing country, another a large producer of coal. One could not assign the oil price shock to explaining the problems of all these countries. Indeed many developing countries, including some with the best records of growth, have no problems with debt or debt-service. The list of countries that pay their debt, as discussed earlier, is much longer than the list of problem debtors. It includes Hong Kong, Malaysia, Singapore, Taiwan, Thailand and many others. For non-OPEC developing countries as a group, estimated debt-service by the end of 1983 was about 20% of exports and not very different from the 1973 to 1979 average of 16%.

The difference in experience, Meltzer argues, reflects mainly two factors. One is the way different countries manage resources and use domestic saving and capital imports (mentioned earlier). The other is the way in which the world community, orchestrated by the IMF and the central banks of the creditor countries, responded to the debt problem in 1982 and 1983. It is not by accident, Meltzer claims, that major debt problems are in Latin America. For decades the United Nations Economic Commission for Latin America (ECLA) urged these countries to restrict imports by using tariffs and quotas of various kinds to substitute domestic production for imports and to promote exports of

---

[4] In a paper delivered at a conference on the International Debt Crisis at the City University Business School (5 Oct. 1983).

manufactured goods. These policies encourage inefficient production, penalise the use of low-cost substitutes and encourage the misuse of resources and waste. When adversity occurs, the least efficient producers have greatest difficulty adjusting and surviving. The rise in oil prices was the shock for Brazil; the fall in oil prices the shock for Mexico; political instability and gross mismanagement the shock for Argentina; the surge in interest rates a shock for all of them. The distinguishing feature is not what happened in the world, Meltzer argues – important as that was – it is what caused *these* particular countries to be so damaged.

During the recent years of high real interest rates, recession, the developing countries of Asia have moved ahead while many of the countries of Latin America have fallen behind. The ECLA programme encouraged inefficient production and since decisions were shifted to a state bureaucracy, it encouraged state planning of investment and production. Considerably more than 50% of the productive assets in Brazil and Mexico are in enterprises owned or directed by government, quasi-government or military bureaucrats. More damaging still, Meltzer argues, is the concentration of planning and decision-making power in a state bureaucracy with power to regulate prices, subsidize production, maintain an overvalued exchange rate and, in these and other ways, distort the use of resources and promote inefficiency.

A recent BIS report illustrated the extent to which debt simply financed "flight capital", i.e. private residents who, fearing political instability and inflation, had acquired foreign exchange and transferred it out of the country.[5]

Table 6.3 shows the proportion of gross capital outflow in relation to foreign debt for selected LDCs:

Table 6.3. Ratio of Gross Capital Outflow 1974-1982 to Gross External Debt at end 1982 (%)

Chile	–5
Brazil	9
Korea	19
Philippines	20
Peru	23
Mexico	42
Argentina	65
Venezuela	90

Source: BIS

[5] See *Time* (10 Jan. 1983)

The BIS claims that Latin Americans had spirited $55 billion abroad in the six years to the end of 1983 – almost a third of the region's increase in borrowing during the period. The $55 billion figure was obtained by subtracting the financing requirement of Latin America from 1978 to 1983 of $130 billion from the increase in external debt during the period – $185 billion. Looked at another way, bad management is illustrated in the case of Zaire. Since 1976 Zaire's debt has been rescheduled at least five times though its debts are small on an international scale – only $5.1 billion. Zaire is a country that has experienced mismanagement and corruption so that it should have represented a warning to lenders. Aside from export setbacks – prices for copper and cobalt have dropped sharply – much of the loan money that flowed in was not spent wisely. Among President Mobutu's development projects was a huge undertaking to drain the Zaire River and to build a one thousand-mile-long powerline to the Shaba copper-producing region, at a total estimated cost of about $1 billion. Eight months after the power was finally turned on, in 1981, the power was switched off. Shaba province was already self-sufficient in electricity. As one Western diplomat commented, "If there was a white elephant this is it. Zaire needs the scheme as much as it needs a nuclear powered submarine".[6]

Mexico incurred a substantial part of its debt to finance investment in oil wells and related projects. Many of these investments were undertaken at a time when experts predicted that oil prices would reach $80 to $100 a barrel by the end of this decade. Instead prices fell and Mexico's investments declined in value.

So mistakes and mismanagement made the problem worse. The Mexican economy is centralized and inefficient. Many of the investment and production decisions are planned by the bureaucrats in Mexico. The Mexican government chose to share its anticipated wealth before it was earned. Transfers and social benefits increased to distribute the oil revenues to the voters and remained intact after the oil revenues declined.

Mismanagement is not confined to local bureaucracies. The policies of the IMF, Melzter goes on to argue, spread the debt problem from one country to another by imposing rules of adjustment that make little sense when applied to many countries.

[6] *Ibid.*

The Fund encourages countries to contract imports and expand exports while at the same time requiring lower inflation as a condition of obtaining loans. The first effect of anti-inflationary policy is on output, so output and imports fall in response to these policies.

Naturally, one country's imports are someone else's exports and in the case of Argentina, Brazil and Mexico linkage is extensive. The combined effect of contraction in Mexico, Argentina and Brazil is a substantial reduction in the volume of trade. Since the three economies are related, they are harmed by each other's policies and still other countries are harmed as well. It is not surprising to learn that many other countries in Latin America, and elsewhere, have lost markets for their exports and needed to borrow from the IMF.

Debt problems in the great majority of cases were also the result of overexpansionary fiscal and monetary policies over a number of years. Although actual conditions differed widely among individual countries, there was an apparently inexorable growth in budget deficits in much of the developing world. For the non-oil developing countries as a group the median fiscal deficit as a proportion of GDP, which averaged 3% in the late 1970s, increased steadily to nearly 6% in 1982. This average conceals some extremely high deficits in a number of countries that ran into debt difficulties including, for example, the three major borrowers in Latin America where the public sector deficits increased from the range of 7 to 8% in 1979 to one of 14 to 18% in 1982. These deficits resulted in strong inflationary pressures and weakening balance of payments positions. They were associated with large external borrowing – much of it at short term – raising debt-service obligations to unprecedented levels in relation to both GDP and exports of goods and services. In many countries, current account deficits eventually became so large as to exceed reasonable financing possibilities.

It is useful to examine the behaviour of a selection of the large borrowers. As Cline and Langoni[7] have shown, throughout the 1970s Brazil consciously followed a high-risk strategy of pursuing high growth based on rapid accumulation of external debt. The resulting legacy of large debt proved to be an oppressive burden

[7] Langoni "The Lessons of the Crises: a Developing Country View", *Euromoney* (September 1983).

when the international economy weakened and exports declined instead of continuing their earlier rapid growth.[8] Matters were made worse by overvaluation of the cruzeiro after an ill-fated attempt to bring down domestic inflation by placing a 40% ceiling on devaluation in 1980.

In Mexico the government allowed the peso to become seriously overvalued and allowed the budget deficit to surge to 16.5% of GNP in 1982 when the upcoming presidential election made authorities reluctant to carry out effective budget-cutting measures. The government adhered to a strategy of high growth (8.2% annual growth in 1979 to 1981) that probably exceeded capacity growth and failed to take adequate account of the substantial weakening of the oil market in 1981.[9]

In Argentina a policy of pre-announcing an exchange rate devaluation by less than the rate of domestic inflation, in an attempt to bring down inflation, led to a vastly overvalued peso, high imports, poor export performance and rapidly rising debt by 1981. Ineffective stabilization policy was followed by collapse of the peso and high inflation. This was compounded by the shock of the Falklands crisis.

THE BEHAVIOUR OF CREDITOR GOVERNMENTS

The direct role of creditor governments in their financial relations with LDCs has been confined to the provision of grants and of aid on concessional terms. They provide aid on a government-to-government basis and through the extension or guarantee of export credits and via their funding contributions to international financial institutions (the World Bank and regional development banks), to the IMF and to United Nations agencies.

Government-to-government aid is by far the most important channel for the disbursement of official aid and member countries of the OECD meet in the forum of the Development Assistance Committee (formed in 1960) to review issues pertaining to the

[8] W. R. Cline, "Brazil's Aggressive Response to External Shock", in W. R. Cline, and Associates, *World Inflation and the Developing Countries* (Washington, 1981) pp. 102–35.
[9] W. R. Cline, "Mexico's Crises: The World's Peril", *Foreign Policy*, No. 49 (Winter 1982–83), pp. 107–19.

scale and flows of official aid. The indirect role of creditor governments, which we shall discuss further on, relates to the economic and financial policies adopted in industrial countries insofar as they have an impact on LDCs.

Foreign aid as an alternative to borrowing – retrospective view

Moral and humanitarian arguments are probably the ultimate, philosophical justification for aid to LDCs but they are supported by an equally strong recognition of self-interest. The real world of aid donor-recipient relationships may never have been quite as former US President Kennedy articulated when he said: "We pledge our best efforts to help them (LDCs) help themselves for whatever period is required not because the Communists are doing it, not because we seek their votes but because it is right". Even if self-interest were an exaggeration of creditor governments' motives for giving aid, there was never a shortage of donors that tried to express a view, militarily or diplomatically, about how recipient governments should be run or conduct their affairs. For foreign aid is essentially a matter of political economy to which economic analysis is subordinated.

After all, the aid programmes of the last thirty years have not helped poor countries escape from the poverty trap nor has it helped them reduce their dependence on aid. Any benefit from aid, moreover, might easily be offset by trade barriers, quotas and tariffs, or concessions regarding the repatriation of capital and profits. Meanwhile, the benefits that flow to the donor from giving aid cannot be ignored. They include political and military prestige and influence and a transfer of political, economic and cultural institutions, installations, patterns and practices to which the recipient country may not be suited. In so doing, however, the donor countries create, however loosely, a network of political and economic satellites which can be counted on for support in terms of political alliances and in terms of the goods and services exported by the donor.

The aid programmes which were developed in the 1950s and 1960s were born of the 1941 Lend Lease programme in which the US supplied wartime assistance to the UK and of the 1947 Marshall Plan in which the US provided for the economic recovery of Western Europe. It is striking to note the clear economic benefits that accrued to Europe from Marshall Plan aid compared with the lack of major improvement in large numbers of LDCs after two to three decades of development aid. Some critics have argued that aid has been more of a hindrance than a help to economic development[10] and that the motives and terms of aid given to LDCs have compared unfavourably with Marshall Plan aid.

One specific distinction made concerns the form of aid given, i.e. the difference between programme aid, which post-war Europe received and which the World Bank has given on a limited scale, and project aid, which most governments have given to LDCs and which may be tied or linked to the donors' benefit.

Project aid enables an account to be kept of what the loan has been used for and permits a relatively strict assessment of the costs, benefits and yields of the project in question. Programme aid, on the other hand, deals in aggregates but is much easier to assess within a wider development planning context. The rationale behind this distinction is that programme aid relates more easily to planning because the process of economic development shows where the resource (savings and foreign exchange) gaps exist and how much is required to fill them. The project approach, however, only looks at individual projects and assesses their costs and benefits without regard for the rest of the economy. For example, a loan to build a railway between a country's mining centres and its ports to facilitate exports (to donor countries) may be a commercially sound proposition. It takes no account, however, of any sudden, unplanned and resulting exodus of people from rural to urban centres, of the spread of shanty-towns and the concomitant social and health problems or of the possibly better application of the loan to road, rather than rail, transportation. Project aid also lends itself more effectively to the practice of procurement, i.e. tying the project loan directly by agreement to the purchase of the donor's exports or non-merchandise services, or indirectly by having donors send instructors and technical experts to work on projects, where they or their trainees will exhibit the same preferences.

In order to address some of the dissatisfaction with the scale and terms of aid, the first United Nations Conference on Trade and Development was held in 1967 and the Group of seventy-seven (subsequently expanded to over one hundred) LDCs resolved to try and promote their economic interests and aspirations uniform-

---

[10] See, for example, P. T. Bauer, *Dissent on Development* (London, 1976), pp. 96–145.

ly, collectively and more firmly. Little of substance came from these, later UNCTAD conferences, or other negotiations. The aid targets suggested by the Pearson Commission's Report (1969) of 1% of each creditor country's GNP were never reached (with some exceptions, mostly in Scandinavia) and they actually declined in the 1970s.

In the 1970s aid became less of a priority for the industrial countries, as their attention turned towards a succession of global economic issues in which their interests were seen to be more direct and more threatened: for example, the collapse of the Bretton Woods system of exchange rates in 1972-1973, the 1973/1974 oil price shock, the 1975 recession and subsequent recovery and the 1979/1980 oil price shock.

In 1981, an independent investigation into the problems of inequality in the world, headed by former West German Prime Minister, Willy Brandt (the Brandt Commission) reviewed the serious shortfalls in official assistance to LDCs and pointed out to industrial countries that "the most urgent need is for the programme of large-scale transfers of funds from North to South to be stepped up substantially. ...". The Commission's views were not accepted universally but in a follow-up report in 1983, it reconfirmed its conclusions and saw official development assistance as remaining the most serious shortfall and the most urgent case for remedial action. Nevertheless, the attitude towards aid among creditor governments has not changed much. Aid-giving in terms of GNP has not been increased and even higher contributions to multilateral official institutions have been either grudgingly and laboriously agreed or reduced. With the proportion of debt owed by LDCs to official creditors around, or less than, half of what it was in 1960, the immediate prospects for change are limited. That this proportion rose in 1983-1984 was more a result of the slowdown in private lending and some increase in IMF lending (see Tables 6.4. and 6.5). Nonetheless, we would argue that creditor governments will have to accept that the international debt situation will not and cannot be resolved without an additional and major supply of public money both to debtor governments directly and to multilateral institutions. Creditor governments can no longer distance themselves from the situation, leaving the debtor countries and the banks to resolve what they cannot. If one or more debtor nations sought to demand access to funds, based not on austerity but on a return to economic growth,

Table 6.4. Non-Oil LDCs:
Sources of External Borrowing.

Sources of External Borrowing (Percentage Share)	1974-1977 (Average)	1978-1980 (Average)	1981	1982	1983
Official Finance	40	30	35	56	69
(i) Long Term Capital	33	29	28	36	47
(ii) Fund Credit	7	2	7	20	22
Private Borrowing	60	70	65	44	31
(i) Long Term Capital	50	47	49	47	79
(ii) Short Term Capital	10	23	16	–3	–48

Source: IMF, *World Economic Outlook,* (1984)

Table 6.5. Non-Oil LDCs: Debt owed to Official
Creditors* as % Total Debt (1983)

By Economic Category		By Region	
All LDCs	31.7	Africa	48.3[1]
(to governments)	(20.7)	Asia	43.9[2]
Net oil exporters	26.7	Europe	29.4[3]
Major exporters of manufacturers	14.9	Middle East	62.6[4]
Low income countries	82.9	Western Hemisphere	17.7[5]
Other LDCs	39.0		
1 Excludes South Africa			
2 Includes China, India, Pakistan			
3 Includes Greece, Turkey, Portugal, Romania, Yugoslavia, Hungary			
4 Includes Egypt, Israel, Jordan, Syria			
5 Principally Latin America and the Caribbean			

Source: IMF, *World Development Report* (1984)
* Excluding multilateral agencies.

creditor governments would not be able to remain on the sidelines, for debtor countries would probably demand relief, in some form from their debt service burdens, to which commercial banks could only accede at some risk to their solvency. In that event, creditor governments would be drawn into the situation, whether they chose to or not.

Although the aid effort of creditor governments has failed to live up to expectations or requirements, governments have reacted to the events that began to unfold after 1982. They agreed in 1983 to increase the IMF's general quotas by over 47% to around $98.5

billion and, at the same time, the group of ten countries together with Switzerland agreed to increase from $6.7 billion to $18.7 billion their commitments to provide supplementary resources for onlending by the IMF under the General Agreement to Borrow (established in 1962). The latter agreement provided for onlending to any IMF member, and not just the group of ten members, as had been the case.

It should be noted that agreement to boost IMF resources was in jeopardy, for a while, as a result of considerable reluctance in the US Congress to ratify the Administration's proposal to contribute an additional $8.4 billion to the IMF.

Some Congress politicians saw the proposed IMF legislation as a way both of tightening controls over the foreign lending of US banks and exerting some political control over the lending decisions of the IMF itself. Independent US bank regulatory authorities sought to stiffen some of the requirements made on banks, in view of Congressional concern that the regulators had not performed their job sufficiently well. In response, the regulators agreed to strengthen the programme for evaluating country risk, obtain increased disclosure of banks' country risk exposure, introduce new rules for accounting for fee income and introduce special reserves for loans to countries with severe and protracted debt servicing problems. Furthermore, the regulators yielded to Congressional pressure and asked the major multinational banks to observe a minimum 5% ratio of capital to assets as an initial step.

Some of the factors which will be deemed to indicate a protracted debt-service problem include a borrower's failure to pay full interest payments on its external debt, or to comply with any restructured terms of indebtedness, or to comply with any IMF (or other suitable) adjustment programme. The special reserves which will be charged against the bank's current income will not be considered part of capital or as an allowance for possible loan losses.

The legislation also makes explicit what sort of IMF lending the US will support or oppose. For example, the US Executive Director of the IMF is to be instructed to oppose IMF credits to any apartheid country and to any Communist country unless otherwise justified by the US Treasury Secretary to the Senate Foreign Relations and Banking Committees and the House Banking Committees. Authorization of such IMF credits will be

given in the case of apartheid countries if the credit would:
- reduce severe constraints on labour and capital mobility through increased access to education or major reform of racially-based restrictions on labour mobility;
- reduce other inefficient labour and capital supply rigidities;
- benefit economically the majority of the population;
- assist a recovery from a balance of payments problem that could not be met by recourse to private capital markets.

In the case of communist countries, authorization will be given if the credit would:
- correct balance of payments difficulties and restore a sustainable position;
- reduce constraints on labour and capital immobility and advance market forces;
- benefit the majority of the population, economically.

On a day-to-day level, creditor governments have begun to play a major role through their central banks. These have played an active part in the debt-restructuring and financial stabilization process, directly (in the case of Mexico) and indirectly, by means of guaranteeing bridging loans (e.g. to Brazil and Argentina) and encouraging their own banks to maintain interbank lines and other credit flows to countries rescheduling their foreign debt – not always successfully. Arguably, however, the current role of central banks is limited to one of trying to extinguish fires wherever they arise rather than of tackling the root cause of the blaze. Central banks can and do attempt to strengthen the infrastructure of the international banking system but, with a very few exceptions, they are generally powerless over such issues as the formulation, as opposed to implementation, of economic policy.

The question about the role of creditor governments is largely a question of responsibility. Specifically we must examine what responsibility they have or should have in the context of economic relations between the haves and have-nots. For a long time after the Second World War and the winning of political independence by former colonial territories, creditor governments believed they had a responsibility to provide development aid to the poorest LDCs and their political allies. Whilst this remains true, the scale of the problem has changed radically. The key responsibility is less concerned with specific aid flows than with the operation and cost of a fairly flexible international economic system, designed to promote economic growth through economic interdependence. In this respect, the economic policies of creditor governments cannot be said to have lived up to this responsibility. The interest payment burden on LDCs cannot be resolved effectively while interest rates, mostly in the US, remain high in both nominal and real terms. This is, therefore, an issue that concerns American fiscal and monetary policies and the Federal budget deficit in particular. The export prospects for LDCs cannot be resolved effectively while economic growth in the West remains subdued and while severe unemployment creates more pressure for trade protectionism. There are simply few votes to be won by opening domestic markets to (low cost) LDC producers.

There is even a certain ambivalence in the policy prescriptions advocated by creditor governments. It is not consistent to advocate IMF orthodoxy as a way out of indebtedness problems because, as more and more countries curtail imports, export markets disappear. It is also somewhat inconsistent to preach monetary and credit restraint as a cure for world inflation and simultaneously to encourage banks to keep lending. The fact that certain events lead to banks becoming the dominant providers of longer-term finance to LDCs is not disputed but the role of banks in this respect was abnormal. This too is recognised but it is a situation which creditor governments are perpetuating.

Chapter 7

The Role of Official Institutions

Several official organisations are key players in the debt game. These include the IMF, the BIS, the Group of Ten and the World Bank. After reviewing the respective roles of these institutions, we look, in a wider context at monetary authorities as "referees" of the international banking system and the issues of lender of last resort.

The role of the IMF

The IMF, currently with a membership of 147 states, exists to promote monetary co-operation as a necessary condition for the balanced and sustained expansion of world trade and, thereby, domestic growth and development. In recent years it has taken an active interest in international debt issues.

In order to help members cope with balance of payments difficulties without resorting to competitive depreciations and restrictions on international trade and payments, the Fund provides financial and technical assistance.

Much of the credit made available to member countries for balance of payments' financing is subject to conditionality. Conditionality refers to the imposition of certain economic adjustment policies on member countries seeking access to the resources of the Fund. Its main objective is "to help members to attain, over the medium-term, a viable payments position, if feasible in the context of reasonable price and exchange rate stability, as well as a sustainable level and rate of growth of economic activity".[1]

[1] Guitian, *Finance and Development* (London, 1980), p. 24.

Under existing policies and practices conditionality is governed by the *Guidelines on Conditionality* (Executive Board Decision No. 6056-(79/38) of March 2, 1979). The most frequently quoted sections of that decision are paragraphs four and nine, *viz:*

> "4. In helping members to devise adjustment programs, the Fund will pay due regard to the domestic social and political objectives, the economic priorities, and the circumstances of members, including the causes of their balance of payments problems.

> 9. The number and content of performance criteria may vary because of the diversity of problems and institutional arrangements of members. Performance criteria will be limited to those that are necessary to evaluate implementation of the program with a view to ensuring its objectives. Performance criteria will normally be confined to (i) macroeconomic variables, and (ii) those necessary to implement specific provisions of the Articles or policies adopted under them. Performance criteria may relate to other variables only in exceptional cases when they are essential because of their macroeconomic impact."[2]

Each of the 147 members of the IMF is assigned a quota based on the relative importance of the member's economy and its share of world trade. The quota has four functions: it determines (1) members' subscriptions to the Fund, (2) within approximate limits the voting rights of members, (3) their borrowing rights on the Fund, and (4) their share of any allocations of SDRs. The quota subscriptions of members are the basic source of finance for Fund lending.

The facilities offered by the IMF are:

- The Credit Tranche Policy is the Fund's basic facility under which credit is available in four "slices" each equivalent to 25% of quota. A distinction is made between the first credit tranche and the subsequent three tranches – the upper credit tranches – to reflect the greater conditionality that accompanies drawings in the higher tranches. The conditionality element is illustrated in table 7.1.

[2] *Selected Decisions of the International Monetary Fund and Selected Documents* (Washington DC, 15 June 1981).

Table 7.1. Possible Tranche Drawings and Related Conditionality

Transaction	IMF Holdings of Members':[1]		Reserve position in the fund (RPF) (% of quota)	Conditionality
	Domestic currency (% of quota)	Reserves (% of quota)		
Deposit of quota	75	25	25	—
Drawings				
Reserve tranche[2]	100	—	—	None[3]
Credit tranche	125	—	—	⎫ Increasingly severe,
Credit tranche	150	—	—	⎬ involving programme
Credit tranche	175	—	—	⎭ agreed by IMF and
Credit tranche	200	—	—	member to overcome balance of payments disequilibrium[4]

[1] Assuming no drawing on special facilities of the Fund and no borrowing of relevant members' currency by other members.
[2] Formerly the gold tranche.
[3] Except balance of payments need.
[4] Performance criteria attached in credit tranches 2-4 only.

Source: G.E.J. Dennis, *International Financial Flows* (Graham & Trotman, 1984).

- The Extended Fund Facility which provides medium-term assistance to help members with structural adjustments in their economies. As above, continued drawings are subject to the fulfilment of performance criteria included in the arrangement.
- The Compensatory Financing Facility which extends credit to members – particularly primary commodity exporting LDCs – with balance of payments' problems caused by temporary export shortfalls largely attributable to circumstances beyond their control. The facility was extended in May 1981 to include balance of payments' problems produced by increases in cereal import costs.
- The Buffer Stock Financing Facility which assists members in balance of payments need to finance their contributions to IMF-approved international buffer stocks of primary products.
- The Oil Facilities which were set up to help members with balance of payments' difficulties owing to the increase in oil prices. Drawings under the facilities ceased in 1976.

- The Supplementary Financing Facility and Enlarged Access Policy which provide resources in much larger amounts and for longer periods than are available under the Credit Tranche Policy or the Extended Fund Facility to members with serious balance of payments' problems that are large in relation to their quotas. These facilities are temporary and may only be used in conjunction with finance from the upper credit tranches or under an extended arrangement. Because these resources supplement those under the Credit Tranche Policy and the Extended Fund Facility, performance criteria apply. Commitments are no longer made under the Supplementary Financing Facility.

While the IMF financial help and expertise have often been major sources of balance of payments' support for individual LDCs with little or no access to commercial sources of funds, cutbacks in private lending to many of the more advanced LDCs have led them to turn to the Fund with the result that IMF financial support is running at record levels as shown in chapter 6.

Unlike the period in the wake of the 1973/1974 rise in oil prices, when a number of special facilities – the Oil Facilities and the Compensatory Financing Facility – with low conditionality were created, current IMF practice emphasizes the need for adjustments. As table 7.2. shows, since 1977 the bulk of the Fund's financial assistance has been provided under facilities that require high degrees of conditionality. On the basis of quotas in effect in mid-1983, an annual limit of 150% of respective quotas, extending over a three year period to 450% was, in effect, tying the provision of financing to progressively more stringent adjustment programmes. Cumulative borrowing, net of repayments, was equivalent to a multiple of six times respective quotas. Drawings under the Compensatory Financing Facility and Buffer Stock Financing Facility, or outstanding drawings under the Oil Facilities, were excluded from these limits.

The Fund's rôle in commercial bank reschedulings is analogous to the part it plays in the Paris Club (see chapter 9) in that it provides information (within the bounds of confidentiality imposed on its relations with members) to debtors and creditors and gives creditors an independent assessment of a debtor's position in the context of its adjustment to prevailing economic circumstances. But there are two important differences. Its participation is not automatic, nor is there necessarily any formal link between

Table 7.2. Low-Conditionality and High-Conditionality Disbursements, 1976-83 (in billions of SDRs) All Members

	Financial Year ended April 30							
	1976	1977	1978	1979	1980	1981	1982	1983
I Low-conditionality	5.09	2.97	0.41	0.64	1.05	1.56	1.65	4.12
First credit tranche	0.29	0.78	0.09	0.13	0.16	0.78	0.02	0.03
Oil facility	3.97	0.44	—	—	—	—	—	—
Compensatory financing facility	0.83	1.75	0.32	0.46	0.86	0.78	1.63	3.74
Buffer stock facility	—*	—	—	0.05	0.03	—	—	0.35
II High-conditionality	0.18	1.78	1.96	0.59	1.15	2.82	5.31	6.14
Credit tranche	0.17	1.59	1.85	0.35	0.93	1.90	2.73	3.68
Extended Fund facility	0.01	0.19	0.11	0.24	0.22	0.92	2.58	2.46
III Total I + II	5.27	4.75	2.37	1.24	2.21	4.39	6.96	10.26

* Less than SDR 5 million.
Source: IMF *Annual Report, 1983*.

rescheduling and Fund-supported programmes (though the debtor is generally urged to negotiate a Fund-supported programme). In practice, the Fund is frequently asked to facilitate reschedulings and commercial creditors have always been influenced by the fact that a debtor has a Fund-supported programme in place.

In practice all the IMF-backed reschedulings have had three essential ingredients: firstly, the commercial banks agreed to reschedule their outstanding debt and to make a modest contribution net new lending; secondly, their lending was supplemented by finance from the IMF and thirdly, the IMF's contribution was conditional on the borrower undertaking austerity programmes.

The Fund has played a very active rôle in a number of recent commercial bank reschedulings involving major debtors. It has adopted a more co-ordinating rôle than before in synchronizing the major commercial reschedulings arranged for some Latin American countries with the establishment of Fund-supported programmes.

Since the Mexican debt crisis broke in 1982 the IMF has found itself involved in loan negotiations with dozens of borrowing countries and hundreds of lending banks. By the winter of 1984 it was supporting adjustment programmes in some sixty-six countries, involving commitments of about $21 billion, of which nearly over half had been drawn. Indeed it is difficult to imagine who, other than the IMF's Managing Director and his expert staff, could have undertaken the necessary mediation. The mediator had to be independent of the parties involved and to command negotiating and financial skills of a high order. Moreover, his ability to reach a settlement acceptable to the lending banks required firstly, that he should have available an official source of finance to supplement what the private sector banks could be induced to contribute and secondly, that he should have the authority to impose politically unpalatable constraints on the borrowing countries' economic policies.

Indeed there were situations in which a failure to act would have harmed not only the members' own adjustment but possibly the functioning of the international monetary system as well. The Fund was able, in these cases, to establish an adjustment programme promptly, based on explicit prior assurances of the availability of future financing from the creditors.

In a recent speech, the Managing Director of the Fund pointed out:

"If the Fund had sought to catalyze additional resources from banks and advocate large-scale rescheduling of repayments the countries in question would have been faced with the need to adjust to far lower levels of financing. This would have entailed extremely high economic, social and human costs, not to mention the danger of destabilizing the financial system, itself inherent in such a situation. After the explosion of bank exposure in several countries since the late 1970s it was important for banks to participate in new financing for 1983 and beyond, but in such a way as to gradually scale down their funding. Thus banking operations recently organized for the three largest Latin American countries show a net increase in exposure of 7% to 8% in 1983, compared with an average of about 30% during 1978-1981."[3]

However, the IMF has not been without its critics. The IMF approach is often viewed as short-sighted and anti-growth. It is argued that it imposes a doctrinaire solution uniformly on dissimilar countries and that it is uncaring about the social and political costs of its prescriptions. The Managing Director himself addressed these questions in a recently-published pamphlet entitled *Does the Fund Impose Austerity?*[4] He pointed out there that while the first results of corrective policies will often be to slow growth performance because of the need for a major reallocation of resources as prices change, countries which persevere with adjustment policies can expect to enjoy more vigorous and more enduring growth as the fruit of incentives and measures to encourage more domestic savings, more investment, more production and more exports.

An increase in IMF quotas

The Interim Committee of the IMF argued in 1982 that the Fund required a substantial increase in resources to allow it to meet the expected growth in demands from the LDCs for balance of payments' support. An average increase of 47.5% in quota subscriptions was agreed under the Fund's Eighth General Review of Quotas, bringing the total to some SDR 90 billion. Despite delays in securing individual legislative approvals, the increase

[3] *IMF Survey* (Oct. 1984).
[4] (1985).

became effective at the end of November 1983 – over one year ahead of schedule. In an attempt to reflect the changing importance of members' relative positions in the world economy 40% of the increase was distributed in proportion to members' existing quotas and 60% in the form of selective adjustments.

As discussed below, the Group of Ten also supplies supplementary financial support to the IMF.

The rôle of the Bank for International Settlements (BIS)

Often known as the central bankers' central bank, the BIS has its headquarters in the Swiss city of Basle. It was set up in 1930 to handle German reparations after the First World War but today provides an invaluable forum for central bankers, handles international monetary transactions, takes deposits from central banks worldwide and monitors the scale and scope of banks' lending and borrowing activities.

The BIS traditionally likes to maintain a low public profile but it has been pushed very much into the limelight by the debt crisis.

Acting through the Basle institution, the developed countries' central banks have been closely involved in various rescue arrangements by disbursing short-term credits and bridging loans to countries such as Hungary, Mexico, Argentina, Brazil and Yugoslavia. The loans are generally intended to bide the borrower over until it can hammer out an agreement with the IMF for longer-term assistance.

Although the bank has ready access to substantial amounts of money *via* its central bank members, it was never intended to assume a permanent rôle as a source of bridging finance. It is reluctant to get involved in rescue efforts to avoid appearing a "soft touch".

It sets strict terms for its loans insisting that they are very short-term and secured against the borrowing countries' assets (usually gold or foreign exchange reserves).

Resolving debt problems is further complicated in that banks operating internationally may have interests in different types of foreign banking establishments. These include branches, subsidiaries and joint ventures or consortia. Branches are operating entities which do not have a separate legal status and are thus integral parts of the foreign central bank. Subsidiaries are legally independent institutions wholly-owned or majority-owned by a bank which is incorporated in a country other than that of the subsidiary. Joint ventures or consortia are legally independent institutions incorporated in the country where their principal operations are conducted and controlled by two or more parent institution, most of which are usually foreign and not all of which are necessarily banks. While the pattern of shareholdings may give effective control to one parent institution, with others in a minority, joint ventures are, most typically, owned by a collection of minority shareholders.

The different organisational systems for international banking means that effective supervision of international banks cannot be limited to unilateral efforts by domestic authorities. It requires a co-operative effort among national supervisory authorities. A major step forward in the area of supervisory co-operation was taken in 1975 with the formation at the BIS of the Committee on Banking Regulations and Supervisory Practices.[5] This Committee was formed by the central bank governors from the Group of Ten major industrial countries, described later, together with Switzerland, to improve the co-ordination of national surveillance of international banking activities. Committee meetings provide a forum for the discussion of the key supervisory and regulatory issues by senior supervisory officials from the major industrial countries. And, perhaps more importantly, they provide an avenue for developing personal working relationships between supervisors which facilitate rapid and effective co-operation should banks experience difficulties.

Effective supervision of international banks rests on two premises. Firstly, national authorities must be willing to co-operate in monitoring the activities of the overseas operations of foreign banks. Secondly, authorities must be capable of supervising their banks' international business.

One of the first tasks of the Committee in 1975 was to develop

[5] This Committee is often referred to as the *Cooke Committee* after Peter Cooke of the Bank of England, its current chairman. A more complete review of the committee's history and its contribution is presented in W. P. Cooke, "The Development of Co-operation between Bank Supervisory Authorities in the Group of Ten Countries, Luxembourg and Switzerland", a paper given at the *International Conference of Banking Supervisors* in Washington DC (Sept. 24–25, 1981).

principles for international supervisory co-operation. In particular, guidelines were needed to ensure comprehensive and co-ordinated surveillance of all foreign banking offices. The general statement of the Committee's views – commonly referred to as the Concordat – was endorsed by the countries represented on the Committee in December 1975.

In dividing supervisory responsibility among national banking authorities, the Concordat distinguishes between the supervision of liquidity and solvency, and between the supervision of foreign branches and legally separate banking subsidiaries incorporated in a foreign country. The supervision of liquidity of all foreign offices and the solvency of subsidiaries is regarded as a primary responsibility of the host-country authorities. Table 7.3. summarises the position.

To be fully effective, the principles set forth in the Concordat need to be endorsed by supervisors worldwide. Acceptance by supervisors outside the BIS-member-countries has spread but no formal endorsements have been made. Further, the effectiveness of the Concordat rests on the capability of national authorities to supervise the international activities of their banks.

If a big international bank experiences serious difficulties, the central bank governors are responsible for tackling the situation. They would use their two principal forums – the Group of Ten and the Bank for International Settlements – as channels for discussion and action.

Both the Group of Ten governors and the BIS directors meet once a month in Basle. Both committees discuss the same problems of international finance and there is an overlap of personnel. But the Group of Ten governors have more global influence, as the Group includes the USA, Canada and Japan, together with the UK, France, Germany, Italy, Belgium, the Netherlands, Sweden, and expanded recently to include previous honorary member, Switzerland. The eight BIS directors are all governors of European central banks (Belgium, The Netherlands, France, the UK, Germany, Switzerland, Sweden and Italy).

An important distinction between the Group of Ten and the BIS is that the Group of Ten is a more political forum as it meets at the behest of the finance minister whereas the BIS represents a more pragmatic banking viewpoint.

Table 7.3. Solvency and Liquidity Supervisory Arrangements

	Solvency Supervision by	
	Parent authorities	*Host authorities*
Branch	*primary* responsibility; solvency indistinguishable from parent bank	general responsibility to monitor financial soundness
Subsidiary	*jointly*, in context of consolidated supervision	*jointly*, as it is a separate entity, legally incorporated in host country
Joint venture	take account of commitment shareholder bank(s)	*primary* responsibility, for practical reasons

	Liquidity Supervision by	
	Parent authorities	*Host authorities*
Branch	need to be aware of parent bank control systems	*primary* responsibility, especially insofar as liquidity is related to local practices and functioning of domestic money market
Subsidiary	should take account of stand-by, other facilities and commitments	
Joint venture		*primary* responsibility

Source:

The rôle of The Group of Ten

The Group of Ten is effectively a subcommittee of the BIS. It is made up of senior central bankers and treasury officials from the 11[6] richest Western countries who meet at the BIS under the chairmanship of Karl Otto Poehl, president of Deutsche Bundesbank, Germany's central bank.

Discussions at the Group of Ten meetings have recently concentrated on three major areas: the need for the IMF to monitor exchange rate movements more actively, how best to harmonize member countries' macro-meconomic policies to foster sustained world economic recovery and ways of ensuring adequate supplies of global liquidity over the coming years.

[6] The Swiss Parliament recently delayed a vote which would finally approve Switzerland's full membership of the Group of Ten. The Swiss have been directly involved in its deliberations and policy formulation, however, for many years.

Under the General Agreement to Borrow (GAB) ten industrial member countries plus Switzerland stand ready to lend to the Fund "to forestall, or cope with, an impairment of the international monetary system". Although by early 1984 the use of the GAB had been limited to the eleven participants, it has now been agreed to make it more flexible by making such resources available to all Fund members, subject to, firstly, the borrower agreeing a major economic and financial programme with the Fund and, secondly, there being deemed to exist a threat to the international monetary system. The amount committed has been increased from SDR 6.4 billion to SDR 17.0 billion and became effective at the end of 1984. An associated agreement allows the IMF to borrow the equivalent of SDR 1.5 billion from Saudi Arabia in parallel with the GAB, while the equivalent of a SDR 3 billion interim financing facility has been agreed for the Fund by the Group of Ten major industrial countries, a number of other advanced countries and the BIS. Saudi Arabia is to match this figure with a further SDR 3 billion.

The rôle of the World Bank

The World Bank or, to give it its full name, the International Bank for Reconstruction and Development (IBRD), is the IMF's sister institution and shares the same 147 members. Unlike the IMF, however, that is until recently, it tended not to get involved in the debtor countries' short- or medium-term economic problems. Instead, it was essentially interested in longer-term development aid (up to fifty years in some cases) which it usually ties to specific industrial or agricultural projects.

In recent years the Banks' lending policies have evolved in an additional way which brings them closer to those of the IMF, especially to the latter's Extended Fund Facility. Though project lending comprises at least nine tenths of the Bank's total lending, it has introduced so-called programme-lending, not tied to specific projects, for the support of development programmes in economies with short-term foreign exchange problems.

The response of the World Bank to the debt crisis has been firstly, to concentrate more heavily on lending activities which support needed macroeconomic and sectoral policy changes, while intensifying assistance to member countries in the analysis, design and implementation of appropriate policies; secondly, to accelerate disbursements and increase the Bank's share of the financing of

new and selected ongoing projects in order to help cushion the
impact of necessary fiscal austerity or the completion of high-
priority investments; and thirdly, to urge other lenders to make
similar efforts. An important vehicle in this latter endeavour is
offered by new methods of co-financing with private commercial
lenders, whereby longer-term/lower interest rate credit is made
available than would be obtained from commercial sources alone.

Monetary authorities as referees

The term monetary authorities may be taken to include creditor
governments, central banks and international organizations. Their
role as referee is deemed to derive from the authority they have to
set credit standards, guide financial relationships through policy
and relax or tighten monetary conditions and, therefore, banks'
ability to lend. Monetary authorities permitted the debt game to
get out of hand by not taking a more active and positive role earlier
and by not defining the new rules of the game. They did not point
out the potential hazards of recycling and turned a blind eye to the
fall in standards of creditworthiness associated with the new
lending undertaken by commercial banks.

The IMF Annual Report for 1976 noted this development for
the first time and casually pointed out that the amount of gross
borrowing required to finance a given external payments deficit
was bound to rise given the increase in debt-service charges.

As this process developed and deepened in the period up to
1982, banks became more and more "locked in" to their sovereign
risk exposures. They could not extricate themselves from their
borrowers without precipitating the actual crises they sought to
avoid and when they did attempt to reduce their exposures after
1982, the monetary authorities sought to restrain them. Had the
authorities acted more firmly and persuasively in the mid-1970s,
the world would have faced a similar economic slow-down and
period of adjustment, but the debt creation would have been
substantially less and the problems created by the debt itself might
have been avoided.

The ultimate rôle of the monetary authorities is or should be to
manage and supervise the banking and financial sectors so as to
prevent a drift or lurch towards financial disturbances. Given the
undesirable consequences of financial crises what choices are open
to the monetary authorities? These can be classified as threefold:

- Do nothing, i.e. no crisis management;
- Invoke lender of last resort facilities;
- Create an international lender of last resort (ILLR).

These will be discussed in turn.

No crisis management

As Kindleberger[7] has illustrated, the notion that a financial panic should be allowed to pursue its course has two strains running through it. One strain takes a certain amount of pleasure in the problems created within the financial market place as retribution for excesses of the past – a somewhat puritanical view.

The other strain welcomes the panic as somehow clearing the air and purifying the financial and economic climate. In practice, neither strain is practical or realistic. Given the undesirable financial and real consequences for participants and non-participants, discussed in chapter 2, other solutions need to be examined.

The lender of last resort

It has sometimes been suggested that the traditional lender of last resort functions of central banks could be invoked to solve the debt crisis. The role of the lender of last resort (LLR) was not respectable among theorists until Bagehot's *Lombard Street*[8] appeared in 1873. The rule laid down by Bagehot was that loans should be granted to all owners on the basis of sound collateral. There is a problem here, however, in that what is sound collateral in stable times can quickly become unsound in a crisis.

In answering the problems of how much should be lent and when it should be lent, Bagehot's rule was that money should be lent freely against sound collateral but at a penalty rate. In this way unsound borrowers will go out of business and sound borrowers will still be there with no rapid decrease in sound economic activity. Bagehot was not without his critics. Perhaps the point made most frequently is that the existence of a lender of last resort creates a problem of *moral hazard* (discussed on pp. 117-19). That is, if the banks know that someone is there to bail them out in a

---

[7] Kindleberger, *Manias, Panics and Crashes: A History of Financial Crises* (New York, 1978).
[8] W. Bagehot, *Lombard Street: A Description of the Money Market* (London, 1873; repr. London, 1917).

crisis they may take more chances – reserve ratios will be lower, dividend payouts will be higher, loans will be riskier – and, as a result, panics will be more frequent than they would otherwise be.

In the case of the USA, the Federal Reserve has shown in recent years, how, in a domestic context it has invoked lender of last resort facilities. Examples include its reaction to the Continental Illinois bank scare, to the growing failures of American banks and savings and loan associations, and to the eleventh hour bail-out for US banks in 1984, when their failure to reach agreement with Argentina would have meant a large increase in banks' non-performing loans and write-offs. The Federal Reserve could do the following to help banks:

- It could increase banks' non-borrowed reserves through open market operations, i.e. buying securities from banks in exchange for cash;
- It could reduce banks' minimum reserve asset ratios, so that banks could realize and use more of their reserves.

Any of these actions would stem the initial rise in interest rates, one of the first signs of financial crisis, and allow them to decline, though much would depend on the manner of the central bank's intervention since any perception that the authorities were acting in an overtly inflationary way might cause interest rates to rise again promptly. What central banks cannot resolve in this way, however, is a solvency crisis. This is because the assets of insolvent banks would not be large enough to raise sufficient cash to meet their liabilities, irrespective of how much additional liquidity is made available. In fact, such a situation would probably not arise since an insolvent bank would not be allowed to trade. The problem would be more serious if several large banks were in this situation because even if the central bank contrived to reduce interests it is unclear whether the problem could be contained. Lower interest rates would raise the value of banks' holdings of bonds, securities and similar assets, but only if the additional liquidity supplied were sufficient to cause a major decline in long-term interest rates. Under present circumstances in the USA this would seem difficult to bring about. In other words, given the size and prospects for the US budget deficit, which is partly to blame for the existing high level of long-term interest rates, a major infusion of liquidity would be seen to be highly inflationary and the market reaction would probably be to sell bonds, causing long-term rates to remain high or rise further. Inevitably, multiple insolvencies among banks would be tackled at the official level with major lender of last resort facilities in order to protect those banks that were the strongest and the most likely survivors. A number of banks, however, would probably be allowed to fail and go out of business, or their more profitable parts would be acquired by competitors with public authorities, i.e. taxpayers and shareholders paying the price for the bad loans and losses.

In one sense there is not too much cause for concern. Multiple defaults or a few major ones would threaten the solvency of some major banks but prompt and proper action by central banks could help to restore confidence and allow threatened banks to resume business on a sounder basis.

The cash provided by central banks to cover banks' remaining losses – after the shareholders had been wiped out – and to inject new capital would probably mean that the central banks or their agents would purchase a going concern at a substantial discount. Most depositors would be protected through deposit insurance schemes or the like. Interest rates would be relatively higher for poorer credit risks and lower for better ones.

At some stage the liquidity injected as part of the rescue operation(s) could be drained out of the system so as not to encourage a damaging revival of inflationary expectations. Any such scenario must involve pain and loss. In this event, the holders of bank shares would be the principal losers but the deflationary consequences of a major threat to the banking system would be containable and manageable.

However, at the international level there are major disparities and gaps whereby lender of last resort facilities would not necessarily resolve the international debt crisis. These have been well summarised by Dale:[9]

"i) When monetary authorities provide financial assistance to commercial banks experiencing temporary liquidity difficulties, there are varying national distinctions made between formalised routine use of the official discount window, and longer-term support operations undertaken on a discretionary basis.

[9] R. Dale, *Bank Supervision Around the World: Group of Thirty* (New York, 1982), pp. 21–2.

ii) Although emergency assistance is typically extended directly by the central bank, there are different alternative methods of support in different countries (e.g. special joint facility of the authorities and the banks; lending below market rates to institutions prepared to acquire or assist the problem bank; general support, with or without official encouragement, by one or more large domestic banks).

iii) Crucially, several financial centres – notably Luxembourg, Hong Kong and Singapore – have no indigenous central banks. (Luxembourg has no LLR at all.) This (and other problems) would appear even more widespread and serious among financial centres not included in the Group of Thirty study (e.g. Cayman Islands, Bahamas).

iv) Frequently emergency support can be offered on a secured basis to solvent institutions. Some countries have broader powers of intervention where insolvency is threatened; elsewhere the deposit insurance agency has LLR power which – for potentially insolvent institutions – may exceed those of central banks.

v) Some central banks are permitted to act as LLR in domestic currency only, although these funds may in principle be converted. Elsewhere, the capacity to provide foreign currency assistance has specific limits.

vi) To varying degrees, countries conceal the precise scope of LLR, as a matter of policy. In general, they expect foreign parent banks to provide all necessary assistance to their local subsidiaries, although the threat of shareholders' actions could limit their commitment.

vii) Finally, where banks do fail, national liquidation proceedings sometimes favour local depositors. (US and many other deposit insurance schemes, too, leave big and/or foreign depositors virtually unprotected.) For this, several countries treat branches of foreign banks as separate entities requiring their own liquidators; such creditors may also enjoy a preferential claim to tranche assets.

In conclusion one cannot rely on the existence of LLR facilities stabilising the international financial system from large 'shocks'."

Do we need an international lender of last resort?

Six trends in international banking since the early 1970s have increased the need for an international lender of last resort (ILLR) and for new forms of international central bank co-ordination and supervision. These have been discussed in earlier chapters and summarised by Griffith-Jones and Lipton.[10]

Firstly, the growing dependence of developing countries on commercial lending, a very high proportion of which has been short-term.

Secondly, the rapid increase in the financing needs of the developing countries.

Thirdly, the rising trend of debt service ratios: by mid-1982 the debt-service ratio (DSR) to annual exports of goods and services was 38% for oil-exporting LDCs, and 24% for oil-importing LDCs as a whole (IMF 1982). In 1965-74, when risks were smaller, difficulties arose in thirty-eight of the 102 cases where an LDC had a DSR above 20% in a particular year, but only in two of the 478 cases with a DSR below 20%.[11] Nor, on past evidence, need recovery – especially if patchy – reduce the risks. For some debtors it could even worsen terms of trade and/or raise interest rates. Hence, there is no validity whatever in popular and populist claims that the international threat to financial stability is somehow unreal, or no greater than before, or that urgent demands for ILLR or other action constitute some sort of "bankers' ramp".

Fourthly, the concentration of bank lending: the debts – and risks – are the more alarming for being highly concentrated on a few big debtors and banks. At the end of June 1982, of $347.5 billion owed by the hundred plus developing countries to BIS reporting banks (excluding offshore centres), some 49.6% was owed by Argentina, Brazil, Mexico and Venezuela (Morgan Guaranty 1983)[12] all of whom in early 1983 had reported DSRs well over 100%. Exposure by the first three alone by the ten leading banks was $38 billion over 40% of the countries' bank debt, and over 140% of the banks' total equity!

Fifthly, the concentration of bank deposits: "recycling" of OPEC funds meant that, by December 1981, 16% of total deposits of private banks in the BIS reporting area originated from the oil-exporting countries; and about 38% of these banks' net external resources (deposits minus credits) came from oil-

[10] S. Griffiths-Jones and M. Lipton, *International Lenders of Last Resort: Are Changes Required?*, Midland Bank Occasional Paper in International Trade and Finance (Mar. 1984).
[11] G. Feder *et al*, "Estimation of Debt Service Capacity Index", (World Bank Washington DC). M. Lipton, "World depression by Third World default?", *Bulletin of Institute of Development Studies* 12 (2 April 1981).
[12] *World Financial Markets* (Morgan Guaranty, 1983).

exporting countries, mainly Saudi Arabia, Kuwait and the UAE.

Sixthly, the changing supervisory needs of the market: the internationalisation of banking – through syndicated lending, with the participation of banks from different countries to finance developing country and Comecon borrowing; the rapid growth of a much larger, international interbank market; a growing search by banks for legal means to avoid exposure limits and to reduce tax liability – has resulted in a great variety of foreign branches, subsidiaries, affiliates, so-called holding companies, etc., largely in offshore centres with parent banks based in other countries. As a result, a large proportion of operations and flows do not clearly fall within the purview of any national supervision of LLR authorities.

As Kindleberger[13] has pointed out, responsibility for international banking stability (like health and welfare) is a public good, even if public provision of it may somewhat diminish private self-reliance. The good is too risky, and fraught with externalities to be provided by one, or even several, private agents acting alone. This approach does not necessarily rest on the perception of some analysts that the US, and other banking systems are inherently fragile, but on the possibility that the international capital market is mostly resilient but can very occasionally break down, with huge, unpredictable, lasting and maldistributed costs.

National LLRs cannot cope with the problems of an international bank. As central banks or other national authorities represent their own national interests, they will be unlikely to take a cosmopolitan view of their responsibility in a crisis – unless, implausibly, potential loss from absence of ILLR and potential cost of ILLR rescue, are in the same ratio for all creditor countries involved. It may be feared that, as a consequence, no single lender of last resort may be willing to save a given bank (whose activities transcend its frontiers) from a liquidity crisis, because the domestic effects of inaction do not seem to be larger than the cost of support, even though the world consequences may be.

Inevitable conflicts of interest will arise where parent banks, subsidiaries, holding companies, depositors and borrowers have varying nationalities. Each central bank will try to minimize its

---

[13] Kindleberger, *Manias, Panics and Crashes: A History of Financial Crises* (USA and UK, 1978). "Distress in International Financial Markets", lecture for the Swedish Economic Association (15 Dec. 1982).

proportion of the costs of any ILLR operation. Delays and disputes about responsibility can themselves reduce confidence and deepen a crisis. However, the case for an ILLR it is argued is weakened by two problems.

Problems of having an international central bank

Two problems, moral hazard and the incentive to free-ride, have been stressed by Heffernan[14] as creating problems for an international central bank (ICB).

Moral hazard relates to the proclivity of individuals to increase the likelihood or size of a risk against which they are insured. In the case of health insurance people may take less care of their health (or call on the service of doctors unnecessarily) if they know the cost of restoring it (or paying the doctor) will be met wholly by the insurer. In theft insurance moral hazard may induce neglect in locking doors or windows or in installing simple safety devices to reduce the risk of theft or the size of the loss if it occurs.

In international banking the presence of an international central bank designated to provide liquidity to solvent banks affects the behaviour of both international lenders and international borrowers. On the lending side moral hazard can arise from two sources. Firstly, the presence of an ICB will alter the risk profile of sovereign loans. Given the possibility of being bailed out, banks may be encouraged to make riskier loans. Secondly, insolvent banks, which should not be bailed out on the grounds that they are inefficiently managed, would have an incentive not to admit this fact thereby maintaining their operations: a socially wasteful exercise.

Heffernan, basing her ideas on those of Guttentag and Herring,[15] stresses that there are gaps between the roles of central banks and an international central bank with respect to their potential responsibilities. In particular the ICB should act to eliminate three types of vulnerable banks, as identified by Guttentag and Herring. These include banks headquartered in countries with, no LLR facilities (e.g. Luxembourg), inconvertible currencies, or a shortage of foreign exchange reserves and also

[14] S. Heffernan, "Reflections on the Case for an International Central Bank", paper presented to a conference at City University.
[15] J. Guttentag and R. Herring, "The lender of last resort function in International Finance" No. 151 (1983), p. 4.

subsidiary banks with ambiguous access to the parent's central bank facilities. The functions of the ICB would be to minimize the number of these gaps.

On the borrowing side the moral hazard problem arises from two sources. Firstly, the ICB facilities change the risk profile associated with sovereign loans. It could increase the incentive of debtor countries to either default, or threaten default, on their sovereign loans. Or, secondly, it could dull their incentives, thereby making them more likely to use these loans for high risk projects.

The ICB, Heffernan goes on to argue, would assume two responsibilities:

"Its first task would be to convince governments of borrowing countries that default probabilities have to be minimized in order to persuade potential lenders to grant loans. The ICB could argue that if lenders perceived a near zero default incentive, the cost of the loan would be lower. Second, the ICB would act as an enforcement body. Member countries would agree that, in the event of default or rescheduling, the country in question would grant economic sovereignty to the ICB until the latter was satisfied all was being done to prevent an exacerbation of debt difficulties. This would also deal with the incentive problem of potentially careless economic management."[16]

Guttentag and Herring also stress special characteristics of international banking that make an ILLR essential. Interbank credit lines may cause one bank's failure to damage the solvency of other banks. Furthermore, several of the largest international banks hold similar assets in their portfolios. Here one bank's weakness may raise suspicions about other banks'. On either ground, failure of one bank may result in deposit outflows from other banks. Thus uncertainties about ILLR may make uninsured depositors more prone to abrupt reassessments of the creditworthiness of banks. This creates, under current conditions, unacceptable risks to the stability of the international banks.

Such authors as Guttentag and Herring recognize the problem of moral hazard, but attempt to overcome it by mechanisms which

[16] S. Heffernan, "The Insolvency of Financial Institutions Assessment and Regulatory Disposition", in P. Wachtel (ed.), *Crises in the Economic and Financial Structure* (New York, 1982).

they perceive as far more efficient (i.e. effective bank supervision). Moreover, if uncertainty is used to control moral hazard, private banks may not know what behaviour would disqualify them from support. They will therefore not know what activities they should avoid. Most important, uncertainty in time of crisis must involve delay, speculation and dangers of further destabilisation – especially if uncertainty is combined with unclear division of responsibility among central banks.

The free-rider problem

The free-rider problem is a well-known phenomenon in group action. Principal actors in a group that take action on their own behalf confer an external benefit on other actors that do not themselves carry out similar action. These marginal actors are "free-riders" in the sense that they participate in a common benefit without bearing any of its cost.

In this case small banks would have an incentive to free-ride. Under some type of resolution of the debt crisis the non-participating smaller banks benefit at the expense of the larger banks without bearing their fair share of the costs. So the benefits of stabilizing the international financial environment may be reaped by these banks without carrying any additional costs. The stabilization may involve "involuntary lending" until normality returns, or participating in the actions of an international central bank.

The standard solution to the free-rider problem is to find ways of marshalling co-operative action by all beneficiaries. Cline has illustrated that there are three basic ways to enforce joint action and overcome the free-rider problem. The first is through official pressure. The IMF is playing an important role here. Nonetheless, there are limits to the use of the official channel to pressure new bank lending. The more compulsory such pressure becomes, the more claim banks will have to official compensation if losses do occur. The second channel for enforcement of collective bank behaviour is the network of influence the large banks have on smaller banks. The large banks can impose retaliatory measures such as exclusion from future syndicated loans or termination of correspondent services. An important third channel is also possible. Banks refusing to participate in a programme of credit extension would no longer be welcome to participate in future lending to the country once more normal times return. Heffernan favours a variant of this latter solution. In order to overcome the free-rider problem the ICB would have to be given authority to exclude non-members from participating in international banking activities.

Heffernan concludes: "To minimize moral hazard and the incentive to free-ride careful monitoring should be conducted by the ICB. The objective should be to monitor new international lending and not to take over existing non-oil developing countries debt".[17]

---

[17] S. Heffernan, "The Insolvency of Financial Institutions Assessment and Regulatory Disposition", in P. Wachtel (ed.), *Crises in the Economic and Financial Structure* (New York, 1982).

Part III
The Game Revisited

Chapter 8
The Rules Change

Fortunately for the LDCs, the stresses which occurred in the early 1970s, discussed in earlier chapters, were alleviated by the simultaneous development of the euro-currency markets to which many major LDCs turned. In so doing, however, they broke some of the traditional rules of the game because the new relationships they formed with eurobanks were of quite a different character to those they had developed with official institutions. In fact there were probably no rules established in this newly emerging game until well after the game had started.

At the same time, i.e. late 1960s and early 1970s, the rules of Bretton Woods were made redundant and obsolete by the crises which led to the failure of that system. The main reason for this was that industrial countries failed to exercise discipline in the pursuit of their macro-economic policies. The most quoted example concerns the financing difficulties encountered by the US in its pursuit of the then President Johnson's "Great Society" social programmes and then, increasingly, in its conduct of the Vietnam war.

The American balance of payments deteriorated and the pressure on the dollar, i.e. on US gold reserves, became so acute that in August 1971 the convertibility of the dollar into gold was suspended. A succession of currency crises proceeded to undermine Bretton Woods rules until the second devaluation of the dollar in February 1973 (the first devaluation was in the December 1971 Smithsonian Agreement on currency par values) gave way to the generalized floating of key currencies.

With the collapse of the Bretton Woods system, the world economy seemed to lose order and certainty. Major currency fluctuations added uncertainty to economic policy decisions and, in the case of LDCs, necessitated the holding of bigger reserves to cope with adverse repercussions on the terms of trade and debt-service costs. Industrial countries no longer had to succumb to the discipline of the fixed exchange rate regime and were able to pursue economic policies independently of their balance of payments position. The framework of international economic co-operation was replaced by a competition among industrial countries, and between them and LDCs, for resources and competitive advantages. The most important and damaging result of the new environment was the inflation which permeated the world economy.

The inflation of the 1970s was a complex phenomenon which was not traceable to a single source and could not be blamed solely on OPEC's decision to raise the price of oil. Rather, the inflation was associated with the pursuit of expansionary fiscal and monetary policies, designed to offset rising rates of unemployment and declining productivity growth. These two latter phenomena resulted from several economic, political and social changes, including the leap in the real price of energy, changes in the composition of the labour force, government regulations affecting the quality of output and working conditions and major increases in public expenditure. These increases, however laudable their objectives were, did have a negative impact on the allocation and efficiency of resource utilization.

They involved the meeting of wide-ranging demands for increases in welfare programmes, agricultural subsidies and assistance to loss-making and competition-sensitive enterprises. The growth of such spending proceeded faster than the rate of economic growth and the growth in tax revenues, so that the imbalance between spending and real output resulted in a steady rise in the rate of increase of prices. Inflationary experiences became translated gradually but firmly into higher inflationary expectations, making the problem even more intractable.

The steady rise in inflation and the maintenance of interest rates well below the level of inflation were a favourable combination for borrowers and an unfavourable one for savers. Borrowers had an incentive to acquire debt because the real value of debt was being eroded by high inflation while savers and lenders into world capital markets became unwilling to commit funds on a long-term basis. The transfer of resources from industrial countries to LDCs could only be accomplished, in the absence of major initiatives from Western governments, through the vehicle of bank credit. Banks were the recipients of substantial new deposits from OPEC countries, which they were eager to lend and the advent of floating interest rates allowed banks to pass on changes in the cost of deposits to their final borrowers.

It might be argued that Western governments encouraged or at least tolerated the rapid expansion of the euromarkets and of international bank lending to LDCs after 1973 because it was in their self-interest for economic growth and import demand in LDCs to be sustained (see Table 8.1). Their major concern at the time was that the oil price increases would usher in a period of world deflation. In lacking the resources and the willingness to play a major role in the resource transfer problem, governments acquiesced in both expansionary economic policies at home and the large-scale intermediation of credit by banks in the international arena. Negative real interest rates, rapid bank credit growth and inflation formed a circle which was allowed to expand and about which governments became complacent. After all, by 1978, the real price of oil had fallen, non-oil producing LDCs had a balance of payments deficit that was below the 1975 level in nominal and, particularly, in real terms, and OPEC's balance of payments surplus had fallen to $2 billion (from $68 billion in 1975). Real interest rates on short-term eurodollars were barely over 1% and of a similar magnitude, or negative, on other major currency instruments.

The problem of inflation, however, was not addressed seriously. Prices and incomes policies were doomed to fail in an environment of rising inflationary expectations, themselves reinforced by expansionary fiscal and monetary policies. Borrowers and consumers gained from inflation and, through their economic activities, reinforced the upward drift in inflation. Governments gained from inflation because it represented a subtle and unlegislated form of taxation to help finance growing budget deficits. Welfare programmes and the indexation of wages and social benefits protected people from the worst effects of inflation.

Yet, the process of inflation was distorting severely the production and allocation of resources and output and discriminating against savings and investment. By the late 1970s, the liberal economic and political order that had prevailed for over a decade looked decidedly shaky and lacking in confidence and a new,

Table 8.1. Non-oil Developing Countries Balance of Payments Sources and Uses of Funds 1973-1983 (in billion US Dollars)

	1973	1974	1975	1976	1977	1978	1979	1980	1981	1982	1983(f)
Use of Funds:											
Current Account Deficit*	11.3	37.0	46.3	32.6	28.9	41.3	61.0	89.0	107.7	86.8	67.8
Net Reserve Accumulation†	10.4	2.7	-1.6	13.0	12.5	17.4	12.6	4.5	21.0	-7.1	7.2
Total	21.7	39.7	44.7	45.6	41.4	58.7	73.6	93.5	109.8	79.7	75.0
Sources of Funds:											
Direct investment	4.2	5.3	5.3	5.0	5.4	7.3	8.9	10.1	13.9	11.4	10.9
Official Transfers	5.5	8.7	7.1	7.5	8.2	8.2	11.6	12.5	13.8	13.2	13.1
Net External Borrowing of which											
Official sources (excl. IMF)	4.9	6.8	11.7	10.5	11.4	13.8	13.3	17.6	23.0	19.5	23.8
Private banks‡	9.8	18.6	23.2	21.5	14.7	25.6	35.9	53.3	52.6	25.0	15.0
											20.0
IMF credit	0.1	1.5	2.1	3.2	—	—	0.2	1.2	5.6	6.3	13.5
Miscellaneous and errors and omissions	-2.8	-1.2	-4.7	-2.1	1.7	3.8	3.7	-1.2	0.9	4.3	-1.3
											-6.3
Total	21.7	39.7	44.7	45.6	41.4	58.7	73.6	93.4	109.8	79.7	75.0

* Deficit on goods, services and private transfers.
† Excludes changes due to SDR allocations and changes in the value of gold.
‡ Estimate of total net borrowing from private banks.
f – forecast
Totals may not add due to rounding.
Source: Adapted from *IMF World Economic Outlook, 1983.*

radically conservative order, proclaiming the virtues of price stability, balanced budgets, rigid monetary control, private initiative and self-help was waiting in the wings. The rules of the debt game were about to be changed again and when oil prices were once more raised substantially in 1979-1980, the response of Western governments could not have been more different from that six years previously. The first and major response was announced in October 1979 when the Federal Reserve of the USA declared its resolve to fight inflation by adopting strict procedures to control directly the growth of the money supply. Other countries also adopted, so-called, monetarist techniques of control and the economic rules changed abruptly.

It is, therefore, with some justification that major debtor nations have voiced complaints of "foul play", i.e. that their financial predicament is to a large extent attributable to circumstances over which they have no control and that major industrial countries changed the rules in their own interests and without regard for the consequences on the ability of LDCs to continue playing the game.

Industrial countries introduce new rules

In the wake of the US monetary policy initative, other key industrial countries adopted a more restrictive monetary policy stance in reaction to the inflation that resulted from the second oil price shock. Interest rates began to increase quickly so that, allowing for the level of inflation, they turned from negative to positive. The terms of indebtedness deteriorated abruptly as the interest cost burden increased. Monetary policies were generally successful in bringing about a substantial decline in inflation over the period 1980-1984 but interest rates did not fall by as much, with the result that real interest rates remained historically high. This was true especially of dollar interest rates.

The financial environment, however, was even more difficult than outlined above. In the US, the currency of which accounts for the bulk of international borrowing, tight monetary policy was accompanied by an expansionary fiscal policy which was the result of the Administration's action in reducing taxes and increasing defence expenditures. The budget deficit rose from less than 1% of GNP in 1979 to 5% in 1984, which was an unfavourable development given that the economic recovery beginning at the end of 1982 was one of the strongest ever. Though other countries ran deficits which were larger in terms of GNP, the US deficit was unique in that it accounted for 55% of net savings. This left little room for the private sector's credit demands to expand without causing upward pressure on interest rates.

Thus, the mix of restrictive monetary policy and expansionary fiscal policy combined to cause a major increase in the level of real interest rates. There were other repercussions. The size of the budget deficit and the prospects of equally big, if not bigger deficits up to the end of the decade made financial markets nervous about the risks of a revival of inflation in years to come. This also caused long-term interest rates to remain higher than they might otherwise have been. The other major result of American economic policy was to produce a substantial appreciation of the US dollar against all currencies. Contrary to regular forecasts that the dollar would fall because of the yawning external deficit that accompanied strong economic recovery, the dollar suffered only minor bouts of weakness between mid-1980 and mid-1984.

Thus, the financial impact of the new rules hit LDC's in three major ways:

(i)   the increase in interest rates (see fig. 8.1) lead to an immediate and sharp increase in debt service obligations and the rise in the level of real interest rates began to threaten the economic viability of development projects if not national economic solvency;

(ii)   the reduction in inflation in industrial countries meant that, in terms of dollars, debt was no longer being amortised as quickly;

(iii)   the strength of the US dollar lead to an immediate increase in the burden of dollar-denominated debt and debt servicing. (See fig. 8.2.)

If these financial repercussions were not serious enough, the real sector results made matters much worse. The combination of restrictive monetary policy and high interest rates produced a major decline in economic activity in the USA and Western Europe between 1980 and 1982. In the latter countries, the downturn was accentuated by moves to close the budget deficits that had grown steadily in the 1970s. The overall impact of these policy measures on LDCs was twofold: firstly, export opportunities were reduced severely because of the weakness of demand in industrial countries and, secondly, as unemployment increased to

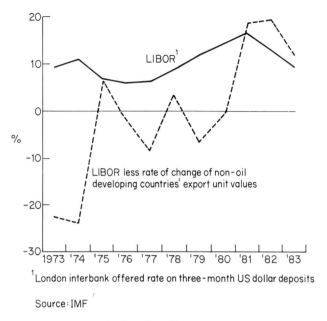

¹London interbank offered rate on three-month US dollar deposits

Source: IMF

Fig. 8.1. Nominal and real interest rates 1973-83

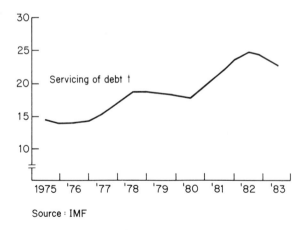

Source : IMF

Fig. 8.2. *Debt-servicing of non-oil developing countries* *+

record levels, protectionist sentiment increased also and LDCs had to confront both cyclical and political pressures on their vital export revenue sources. The new economic policies of industrial countries, therefore, had a pincer effect on LDCs: restrictive financial policies increased the burden of debt and debt repayment (see Table 8.2) while low economic activity and protectionism constrained the opportunities to compensate through increased export earnings (see Table 8.3). They also had a serious impact on banks, partly through the resulting deterioration on the quality of the banks' loans to LDCs but also through the substantial volatility in financial markets and through the deterioration in the quality of banks' domestic assets. There was indeed a certain irony in 1983-1984 in Western governments preaching the virtues of monetary control and domestic credit restraint and urging the banks to sustain or increase their exposure to the most heavily indebted and troubled LDCs.

The greatest irony of all, perhaps, is that the new rules of the game have resulted in the poorer countries in the world becoming capital exporters (i.e. paying more in debt-service than they receive in new loans) and in the richest country in the world, the US, becoming a net capital importer.

Coping with new rules

Debtor countries might argue justifiably that the rules were changed so radically that they could not have prepared themselves for the consequences. Indeed, in his study "International Debt and the Stability of the World Economy", William R. Cline,[1] a senior fellow at the Washington-based *Institute for International Economics*, showed that the external debt of the non-oil producing LDCs increased $482 billion between 1973-1982, to a total of $612 billion.

He estimates that $260 billion of the increase can be attributed to the increase in oil prices since 1974. A further $41 billion resulted from the sharp rise in dollar interest rates in 1981-1982; another $21 billion from lost export volume owing to the worldwide recession and $79 billion from the drop in commodity prices and other terms of trade.

[1] W. R. Cline, "International Debt and the Stability of the World Economy" (Institute for International Economics, Sept. 1983).

Table 8.2.
Developing Countries: Debt-Service Payments and Ratios

(billion US dollars; ratios in per cent)

	1977	1978	1979	1980	1981	1982	1983	1984*	1985*
All developing countries									
Value of debt-service payments	39.8	57.7	75.4	89.6	109.3	124.1	111.7	121.3	142.9
Interest payments	15.4	21.9	32.3	45.8	60.6	71.4	65.1	71.5	80.7
Amortization†	24.4	35.8	43.1	43.8	48.7	52.7	46.7	49.8	62.2
Debt-service ratio‡	15.1	19.1	19.0	17.4	20.2	24.4	22.1	21.5	23.0
Interest payments ratio	5.9	7.3	8.1	8.9	11.2	14.1	12.9	12.7	13.0
Amortization ratio†	9.2	11.8	10.8	8.5	9.0	10.4	9.2	8.8	10.0
Of which major borrowers									
Value of debt-service payments	17.0	26.3	35.7	40.0	52.0	61.6	53.3	55.1	65.7
Interest payments	6.7	10.2	15.6	22.9	30.6	38.7	34.9	38.2	42.0
Amortization†	10.3	16.0	20.1	17.1	21.4	22.9	18.5	16.9	23.7
Debt-service ratio‡	24.8	33.7	35.2	19.7	33.6	44.1	38.8	35.5	37.9
Interest payments ratio	9.9	13.1	15.4	17.0	19.7	27.7	25.3	24.6	24.2
Amortization ratio†	15.0	20.6	19.8	12.7	13.8	16.4	13.4	10.9	13.7
Non-oil developing countries									
Value of debt-service payments	35.8	51.8	66.6	77.4	98.1	109.7	98.9	107.2	124.2
Interest payments	13.7	19.2	27.5	39.4	55.2	63.9	59.0	64.7	71.7
Amortization†	22.1	32.6	39.0	38.1	42.9	45.8	39.9	42.5	52.5
Debt-service ratio‡	16.1	19.8	19.7	18.1	21.4	25.0	22.3	21.7	22.7
Interest payments ratio	6.2	7.3	8.2	9.2	12.1	14.6	13.3	13.1	13.1
Amortization ratio†	9.9	12.5	11.6	8.9	9.4	10.5	9.0	8.6	9.6

* Projections by IMF staff.
† On long-term debt only. Data for the period up to 1983 reflect actual amortization payments. The estimates and projections for 1984 and 1985 reflect scheduled payments, modified to take account of actual and pending rescheduling agreements.
‡ Payments (interest, amortization, or both) as percentage of exports of goods and services.
Source: *World Economic Outlook, September 1984.* Revised Projections by the Staff of the International Monetary Fund

Thus, $401 billion of the $482 billion increase may be attributed to the impact of events over which the debtors had no control. Debt-service problems resulted from a combination of adverse external factors that included high interest rates, declining terms of trade, weak growth and recession in their major industrial country export markets and a proliferation of protectionism. Because of the substantial rise in export volume that was needed to alleviate debt-service problems, and because of the barriers imposed on their export prospects, debtor countries were forced to adjust to the increase in the real resource costs of debt-servicing through cutbacks in imports and in real income – the more so as lines of credit were withdrawn or reduced. (Similar to an owner-occupier who, unable to earn more, can only meet mortgage obligations by

Table 8.3.
Impact of the changes in rules for non-oil LDCs 1974-1983

Changes (%) in:	Average 1974-79	1980	1981	1982	1983
Real output	5.4	5.0	2.8	1.5	1.6
Export volume	5.6	9.0	7.8	1.7	5.3
Import volume	5.7	6.8	3.1	–8.3	–0.6
Terms of trade	–1.1	–4.3	–5.1	–3.5	1.1
Levels ($ billion or %) of:					
External debt*	265.2	475.2	559.6	633.3	668.6
Debt/GDP	25.8	23.9	27.1	32.5	36.7
Debt/exports	121.4	111.2	122.5	144.1	149.5
Debt-service payments	37.5	73.4	97.2	107.7	96.6
Debt-service ratio	16.5	17.2	21.3	24.5	21.6
3 mo eurodollar rate (nominal)	8.5	14.2	16.9	13.3	9.7
3 mo eurodollar rate (real)	–0.8	0.8	7.6	9.3	8.1

Memorandum: For Major Borrowers

Changes (%) in:	1977	1978	1979	1980	1981	1982	1983
Real output	5.5	5.4	5.0	4.3	2.3	0.9	0.3
Export volume	18.3	11.0	33.1	32.1	1.1	–8.0	0.1
Import volume	16.6	16.4	24.0	28.6	9.7	–10.3	–11.5
Terms of trade	3.8	–5.2	6.6	6.2	–2.8	–3.4	0.8
Levels ($ billion or %) of:							
External debt*	256.0	311.9	370.9	440.1	514.3	576.4	606.9
Debt/GDP	27.6	29.1	28.2	27.8	30.7	36.7	42.5
Debt/exports	153.0	163.9	147.4	133.2	150.1	182.3	194.0
Debt-service payments	32.0	42.9	57.6	71.0	93.6	102.1	93.4
Debt-service ratio	19.1	22.5	22.9	21.5	27.3	32.3	29.9

Source: IMF, *World Economic Report*, various.
* After 1980, includes short-term debt, or, in the case of major borrowers, all years.
Note
Non-oil LDCs exclude member countries of OPEC. Major borrowers comprise Algeria, Argentina, Brazil, Chile, Colombia, Egypt, Hungary, India, Indonesia, Israel, Korea, Malaysia, Mexcio, Morocco, Nigeria, Pakistan, Peru, Philippines, Portugal, Romania, S. Africa, Thailand, Turkey, Venezuela, Yugoslavia.

cutting back on a range of expenditures. He then acquires, somehow, an overdraft facility that grows and grows until the bank calls in the overdraft, leaving him just as short of cash but with a bigger debt burden than he can ever hope to repay or service until or unless he can earn a more stable and larger income.)

In order for debtors to secure a net positive financial inflow, they must receive a volume of new loans that is equal to, or greater than, their debt-service commitments. However, if the real rate of interest is greater than the rate of growth of GDP, which it was after 1979 and still is, the debt burden must increase. As and when banks became wary of this deterioration and resisted additional lending and exposure, countries could only service their debts by generating more cash, i.e. turning their balance of payments deficits into surpluses. This many countries duly did but running a payments surplus now meant that debtor nations were transferring real resources to creditor banks and institutions simply to service debt through the mechanisms of domestic austerity.

These were rules to which debtors were totally unaccustomed and which were, in the context of haves and have-nots, distinctly unfair. It is now a matter of great importance and urgency to reflect on whether debtor countries will continue to be willing to make such transfers, over what period, and on what and whose terms. For the costs to them of doing so may soon become, if they are not already, much greater than in failing to do so and passing the adjustment burden to the banks and to creditor governments.

The central issue here is the rule that determines the balance between balance of payments adjustment and balance of payments financing. The costs of adjustment are determined by both debtor and creditor nations through the economic environment which they create and the implications for countries that run external surpluses or deficits. The economic environment created by industrial countries determines the terms on which debt is serviced, that is, either through an expansion of LDC exports at a higher level of real income for LDCs or through austerity and import cutbacks at lower levels of real income. Thus, the redefining of rules in the future is as much a political and a moral issue as it is one of economics and banking.

Part IV
The Stakes

Chapter 9

Debt Rescheduling and the Risks of Default

The issue of debt defaults by sovereign borrowers is about as old as the international banking system itself. Its significance in the 1980s, however, derives from the number of sovereign borrowers with severe financial problems, the size of sovereign debts involved and the unique interlocking of private commercial banks with sovereign borrowers in which the lenders have no real means of enforcing repayment of loans and the threat of debt repudiation carries grave implications for the viability of banks and for the international economic and financial system. Historically, sovereign debt defaults involved either government-to-government loans or loans made (e.g. through bond purchases) by private investors. Where banks were involved, the repercussions were limited and isolated.

In the nineteenth century, as we discussed in chapter 3, several newly independent countries defaulted on their bond issues and/or their foreign debts, including Turkey, Egypt and several Latin American countries. Even in continental Western Europe and in the USA there were many instances of default. Denmark declared default in 1813 because of its inability to repay debts incurred during the Napoleonic wars and, during the remainder of the century, there were five instances of default by German states, five involving Austria and around eighteen involving the Netherlands, Spain, Greece, Portugal, and Russia. In the USA the states of Maryland, Pennsylvania, Mississippi and Louisiana also defaulted on all or part of their loans. What made debt problems unique relative to those of the following century was the recourse by creditors to force repayment of debts due, either through heavy diplomatic pressure that fell just short of military force, or through gunboat diplomacy, usually involving the blockade of ports and/or the seizure of liquid assets. Military force, for example, was used by Britain against Egypt, by France against Turkey and by Spain against Colombia (specifically the blockade of Cartagena, scene of the Latin American debtors' conference in 1984).

The world's major creditor powers, however, were in a position to exert substantial (colonial-style) pressure on a whole range of countries, including China, Serbia, Persia, Bulgaria, Portugal, Greece, Guatamela and Peru.

There were two cases of default at the beginning of the twentieth century, in Venezuela and the Dominican Republic, but the biggest shocks were those involving Russia, where the revolution resulted in bond holders possessing worthless claims and in Germany, which rescheduled its external debts in 1921, 1922, 1924 and 1930, before suspending payments in 1931 and repudiating its debt altogether in 1933. In the 1930s, moreover, some seventeen Latin American nations defaulted on their bond obligations.

After the Second World War economic reconstruction and recovery was assisted by the creation of a new financial order which endeavoured to resolve, amongst other things, the difficulties that contributed to the debt problems before 1939. The immediate post-war years were concerned mainly with the settlement of war debts owed to the USA on a government-to-government basis. The vast majority of the debts incurred by sovereign borrowers in the 1950s and 1960s were from official institutions. Private lending, for example, for the purposes of export financing was limited and tended to be government-guaranteed. It should be stressed again that private commercial banks had a very small role in the financing of the economic development of LDCs until the early 1970s. To the extent that there were debt reschedulings, they involved only governments. Indeed, the first multilateral debt reschedulings occurred in 1956 when creditor governments, meeting as the newly constituted Paris Club, restructured trade debts and insured suppliers credits with Argentina.

How do pre-war and post-war borrowing and lending arrangements compare?[1]

Several important differences between the pre-war and post-war lending arrangements for eastern Europe and developing country borrowers with important consequences for rescheduling have been stressed by Dale and Mattione.[2] Most importantly:

- Short- and medium-term bank lending at floating interest rates has largely replaced fixed-rate bond financing.
- In addition, banks' lending spreads (the margin above their cost of funds) have typically been far below the risk premiums previously demanded by bondholders. This in turn reflects how banks now respond to debt-servicing problems. Instead of agreeing to partial debt relief, as they used to, they stretch out debt repayments on market terms and thereby avoid having to book losses on their loan portfolios. The ability of banks to negotiate collectively with borrowers has made such rescheduling much easier.
- The IMF's third-party role in renegotiations is also a major departure from previous institutional arrangements.
- Finally, the consequences of serious debt-servicing interruptions have become more global since the Second World War because of changes in the creditor-borrower relationship. Firstly, the credit standing of all public-sector borrowers within the same country is now linked. This is a result of central government guarantees on foreign debt and cross-default clauses that have been introduced in loan agreements. (Under cross-default clauses a country may be considered in default on all its loan agreements if it defaults on any one of them.) Secondly, the dependence of country borrowers on the renewal of short-term bank credits has introduced a new source of instability by making the international lending system vulnerable to credit withdrawals, from both countries and geographic regions, when confidence is shaken. Thirdly, the involvement of banks in foreign lending has created direct links between domestic banking systems and country borrowers that could affect Western economies profoundly, if defaults were to occur.

[1] Appendix 9.1 illustrates how game theory applied to this section.
[2] R. Dale and R. Mattione, "Managing Global Debt", Brookings Discussion Paper in *International Economics* No. 3 (June 1983).

Why do countries have debt-servicing problems?

A country may run into debt-servicing difficulties for a number of reasons:

- it may have pursued inadequate macroeconomic policies leading to balance of payment problems undermining its ability to service debt;
- it may have borrowed excessively, that is beyond its current capacity to service the debt;
- it may have borrowed on unfavourable terms (for example, it may have accumulated too much short-term debt) or it may have built up an unfavourable maturity profile, with a "hump" in repayments falling due;
- it may be affected adversely by events that it cannot control. By 1984 over a third of total non-oil developing countries debt was subject to variable interest rates, compared with less than one tenth in 1972. These rates may increase sharply for reasons that have nothing to do with conditions in the debtor country. Also, for reasons beyond its control, the country may experience a temporary but substantial export shortfall reducing its debt. The export shortfall may be due to unfavourable climatic conditions or developments in the world market for the export commodities of the debtor country. Finally, for reasons that may be partly related to developments in a neighbouring borrowing country, new bank lending may suddenly be reduced creating difficulties for another borrower; and
- the country may, for other reasons, find its ability to earn foreign exchange suddenly reduced. In actual practice, several factors may be present, even though one may predominate. Economists and bankers, as discussed earlier, sometimes distinguish between two broad types of debt difficulty: that owing to liquidity problems, defined as a temporary shortage of foreign exchange resources, and difficulties owing to solvency problems, where the debt-servicing obligations are beyond the longer-term economic capacity of the country in question. In practice, elements of both may be present and a solution to a debt-servicing problem must be considered not in isolation but in the context of restoring balance of payments viability.

What can a country do when it cannot repay its debts

A country facing debt-servicing difficulties has, broadly speaking, three choices:

Cease repayments

It may *cease repayments* on its debt and thus accumulate debt-service arrears. Such an action, however, has serious drawbacks. In the case of bond issues, a default may have serious consequences for the state's future access to the bond markets. Prospectuses often contain a statement as to the issuer's debt record. Stock Exchanges may require such a statement. It would be difficult to market an issue in the event of unremedied default being disclosed. Indeed Stock Exchanges may not even admit a security to listing if the debtor is in default on other relevant debt. Two points, however, need to be made here: firstly, the financial sanctions can be mutual. As Lord Keynes is said to have remarked: "If you owe your bank manager a thousand pounds you are at his mercy; if you owe him a million pounds, he is at your mercy". Secondly, in practice many states still in default have nevertheless been able to borrow in the international markets, e.g. the USSR, Bulgaria and China.

A further sanction could be that creditors may directly intervene in the affairs of the defaulting country. Indeed, as Wood illustrated, prior to the Second World War, direct intervention by foreign powers in the financial administration of insolvent states and the appointment of customs or other receiverships was not uncommon.[3] The measures included participation by bondholder representatives in the financial agencies of the debtor state, the establishment of foreign financial commissions, and receiverships of customs duties and other revenues.

Classic examples were the Ottoman Debt Council (1881-1944), controlled by foreign allied powers and the Egyptian Caisse de la Dette Publique (1880-1940), instituted initially by five European powers and performing functions similar to a trustee in bankruptcy. Other debtors subjected to foreign financial control included Tunis (1869), Greece (1898) and Morocco (1902).

Borchard and Wynne illustrate how the US established customs

[3] P. Wood, *Law and Practice of International Finance* (New York).

receiverships in respect of Santo Domingo (1907), Haiti (1916), Nicaragua (1911), Panama, Cuba and Liberia.[4] International financial control was established by the League of Nations over some of the lesser European states in the inter-War period, especially Austria, Hungary and Greece.

It must be stressed, however, that much of this intervention was motivated by political considerations rather than to protect bondholders. In the post-colonial period such intervention is politically unacceptable and is unlawful, e.g. as in the military intervention in Mexico (1861) and Venezuela (1902). These actions have been replaced by more orderly intervention through the IMF stabilization programmes.

There is the further possibility (although rarely a reality) of the country being formally declared "in default", in which case that country's assets abroad (ships, aircrafts, commercial bank deposits, typewriters, *etc*). in foreign tourist offices, may be "attached" or confiscated and sold to discharge the debt. They could not and would not, however, have recourse to a borrower's most valuable assets, its foreign exchange and/or gold reserves and domestically-owned physical assets.

A state which repudiates its external debt is effectively deciding to sever all financial links with the major portion of the international community. Its access to future credit from usable currency sources will tend to be curtailed, it will be deprived of the benefit flowing from membership of the Bretton Woods institutions, and its external assets will be liable to foreign attachment.

A state which refrains from orderly negotiations with creditors may incite creditor suits in foreign courts. In either case, the state cuts itself off from capital and the possibility of universal trade unimpeded by manoeuvres to avoid creditor suits becomes impossible. Dr. William Cline of *The Institute for International Economics* asserts confidently that: "Foreign creditors could attach any of the foreign assets of a defaulting country, as well as its exports abroad (commercial airlines, ships, bank accounts, shipments of commodities, and so forth)".[5]

However, as a recent article in the *Financial Times* noted[6], there

---

[4] Barchard and Wynne, *State Insolvency and Foreign Bondholders* (Yale, 1951), Vols I and II.
[5] W. R. Cline, *International Debt and the Stability of the World Economy* (Institute for International Economics, Sept. 1983).
[6] A. Kaletsky in *Financial Times* (25 June 1984).

are several general problems with sovereign lending which make legal redress extremely difficult. These relate to legal jurisdiction, sovereign immunity and enforcement.

Legal jurisdiction:

If a loan agreement is made under Brazilian or Nigerian law, there is nothing to stop these countries introducing new legislation to make the debt uncollectable, for example by imposing exchange controls or converting debts into local currency. Courts throughout the world will generally judge such agreements on the basis of the laws under which they were made. For example, an English court which was asked for a judgement against Nigeria in such a case would apply the current law in Nigeria, not the law of England.

Fortunately for the bankers, this loophole, which was widely abused by sovereign debtors in the waves of defaults which occurred in the 1930s, 1870s and 1820s (discussed earlier), is of limited relevance today. Most medium-term lending contracts are made either under New York law (for dollar loans to Latin America) or English law. Private trade credits, however, usually are subject to local governing law.

Sovereign immunity

Until recently an insuperable obstacle to litigious creditors was the doctrine stated by the House of Lords: "To cite a foreign potentate in a municipal court is contrary to the law of nations and an insult which he is entitled to resent". It was only with the passage of the Foreign Sovereign Immunities Act of 1976 in the US and the State Immunity Act of 1978 in Britain, that the rights of private litigants were fully recognized. These Acts made it possible for foreign nations to waive their immunity from suits in American and British courts; and such waivers have since been included in most loan agreements.

Colombia, Venezuela and Brazil have sometimes refused to sign such waivers on constitutional grounds but even in these cases alternative wordings have usually been agreed. Thus, most lawyers believe that a default judgement against a foreign government should normally be possible today. They are less sanguine, however, about *enforcement*. It is almost impossible to appropriate foreign exchange owned by central banks. So, as Kaletsky goes on to say, "What about those ships, airplanes and wheat

cargoes?".[7] Most of a debtor nation's overseas assets will belong
not to the Government itself but to various private and public
trading companies. Unlike the government of Iran, which had its
stake in Krupp GMPH attached by Morgan Guaranty during the
1980 hostage crisis, the Brazilian or Argentine governments do not
own major foreign assets in their own name.

In addition, nationalized corporations, fully owned by governments, have separate legal personalities and cannot be drawn into
suits against the government which owns them. Even the state
trading organisations in communist countries have normally been
recognized as legally distinct from their government by both US
and English courts. A country's trade could be further protected
simply by ensuring that the legal title to oil or wheat cargoes
passed immediately to the foreign importer. Much trade is already
done in this way – Mexico's oil, for example, becomes the legal
property of the foreign oil companies which buy it the moment it
enters their tankers.

The sanctions against Iran in 1980 and Argentina in 1982
demonstrated that US politicians (note: *not bankers*) have considerable powers to seize assets or embargo trade. It is unlikely
that these powers would be used on behalf of bankers as they
would simply provoke retaliation against foreign owned companies within their countries.

Ceasing repayments, while legally difficult to enforce penalties
against, would most certainly, however, make life uncomfortable
for future transactions with trading partners.

Debt repudiation, so-called or by any other name, would be a
political decision taken by one or more debtor governments on the
grounds that:

- the country was in any case a net exporter of capital owing to
  the excess of debt-service over new borrowing;
- the decline in living standards had gone far enough and further
  austerity might cause serious social and political upheavals;
- the cost of withdrawing from the international financial system
  in terms of foregone access to bank credit would be less than the
  economic, social and political costs of struggling to earn enough
  foreign exchange to keep interest payments to banks current and
  on time;
- creditor governments would probably come to the aid of both

[7] *Ibid.*

banks and LDCs, albeit at the eleventh hour, in order to avert the worst aspects of the debt crisis and initiate a long-term solution enabling countries to pay.

The main cost of withdrawing from normal international banking relations lies in the closed-off access to trade and other credits. However, debtor governments also know that some credit could probably be obtained from non-western creditors, while trade on a credit basis would be replaced, to some extent, by trade on either a cash or a barter basis. Working out the costs and benefits of alternative strategies may, in the end, be overtaken by a much simpler political question, i.e. whether debtor governments can win back falling popular support and stem domestic political unrest by re-ordering economic priorities and advising the banks that they "can't pay, won't pay" – at least for the time being. Legal opinion as to the likelihood of default was given by Borchard and Wynne:

"The bankruptcy equivalent for a foreign state itself is the purported declaration by its government of a moratorium on the payment of indebtedness, external or otherwise, or other public admission by that government of an inability to pay indebtedness when due. A sovereign government's moratorium could also purport to affect debts of government-owned corporations and . . . even the debt of private corporations. An event of default for a purported foreign government moratorium is . . . probably too extraordinary an event to be much protection to the lender . . . Thus, it is sometimes surprisingly omitted (from the terms of loan agreements)."[8]

Service its debts

Another option may be for the country to try to service its debts at all costs. But to do so it may have to restrict its other foreign exchange expenditures which generally means a reduction of imports – a difficult task in many developing countries where imports already consist of essentials. On both economic as well as social grounds, this may not be a viable course.

[8] R. H. Ryan Jn., *"Defaults and Remedies under International Bank Loan Agreements"*, *University of Illinois Law Review*, No. 1 (1982).

Reschedule

The country may seek a rescheduling, i.e. rearrangement of the repayment terms of their original loan. (It may also seek refinancing which, technically, is different in that it involves a new medium-term loan in the amount of the debt due, which is repaid with the proceeds of the loan.)

A rescheduling may cover the principal only of the principal and interest on repayment falling due in a particular period (usually one year). The rescheduled debt may include a grace period and a stretched repayment schedule. For instance, if repayments falling due in 1986 amount to $100 million and the country succeeds in arranging a rescheduling with a grace period of three years and a repayment period of five years, this means that the repayment falling due in 1986 will be made during the years 1989-1994. Rescheduling thus is not merely postponing a debt, it is spreading over a number of years payments that were due in one particular year. There is, of course, a cost involved in that the debtor country must pay interest on the amount outstanding until the debt has been finally and fully repaid.

The rationale for a rescheduling is to provide time: in cases where the debt problem is due to a temporary foreign exchange shortfall, rescheduling gives time for the balance of payments to improve; in cases where the problem is more fundamental, rescheduling lightens the country's burden and gives time for appropriate corrective measures to be taken in order to improve the balance of payments. In this latter case it is important to recognize that rescheduling is not a panacea and cannot work in isolation: it can only succeed if it is accompanied by steps to address the underlying economic problems.

So the effect of a rescheduling is a sort of *quid pro quo* between the debtor and creditor. The debtor receives a grace period before principal payments have to be made; the creditor receives a higher interest rate or spread over LIBOR on the rescheduling debt and he receives management and other fees which are amortised usually over a shorter period – tantamount to an even higher interest rate. Whilst the country will continue to need a sufficient amount of new borrowing, its ultimate objectives must be as follows:

- to stretch out the maturity of debt, perhaps to twenty to thirty years;

Table 9.1. Multilateral Debt Renegotiations, 1974-83

	1974	1975	1976	1977	1978	1979	1980	1981	1982	1983[1]
Argentina			C							©
Bolivia						C	C			
Brazil										©
Central Afr. Rep								P		
Chile	P	P								©
Costa Rica									P	©
Cuba										©
Ecuador										C
Gabon					P					
Ghana	P									
Guyana						C			C	
India	A	A	A	A						
Jamaica						C		C		
Liberia							P	P	C	
Madagascar								P	P	©
Malawi									P C	
Mexico										©
Nicaragua							C	C	C	
Pakistan	A							A		
Peru			C		P C		C			
Poland								A	C	©
Romania									P C	P
Sengal								P	P C	©
Sierra Leone				P			P			
Sudan						P		C	P	P
Togo						P	C	P		P C
Turkey					A	A C	A		C	
Uganda								P	P	
Yugoslavia										©
Zaire			P	P		P	C	P		
Zambia										P

	In millions of US dollars									
Total amount:[2]	1,530	375	1,800	240	1,800	6,200	3,750	2,540	10,000	37,000

Sources *World Bank, Debtor Reporting System* and data compiled by IMF staff
Notes This table does not include some cases for which sufficient information was not available

P = Paris Club Agreements A = Aid Consortia Renegotiations
C = Commercial Bank Agreements © = Under negotiation with commercial banks at the end of May 1983

[1] As of end-May 1983
[2] Estimates
Source: *Finance & Development* September 1983

- to benefit from lower interest rates, both in nominal and real terms;
- to receive concessional aid to help refinance private non-concessional loans;
- to benefit, perhaps, from a rise in world inflation which would reduce the present value of debt;
- to realize either a strong and sustained trade surplus or to close the deficit and secure more stable, long-term capital inflows.

The rescheduling process has generally covered two types of debts: official debt, that is, loans provided or guaranteed by governments or official agencies and commercial bank debt. Official debt reschedulings are generally handled through "creditor clubs", the best known of which is the Paris Club.

On occasion, official debt is also negotiated through aid consortia, under procedures similar to the creditor clubs.

Commercial bank debt is renegotiated under more *ad hoc* arrangements involving large and often changing groups of creditor banks. An indication of the number and amounts of debts renegotiated in the period 1974-1983 is given in Table 9.1.

OFFICIAL DEBT RESCHEDULING

Paris Club operations

The Paris Club came into being in 1956 when a number of European countries met to renegotiate outstanding balances in their bilateral accounts with Argentina. Since then it has become the major forum for rescheduling official debt. By the end of 1982 at least sixty multilateral debt renegotiations had been held under its aegis, involving at least twenty countries (several more than once). The Club meets at the request of the country seeking to reschedule its external debt. It brings together as many of the official creditors as are willing to participate. Under an informal arrangement, the meetings are chaired by a senior official of the French Treasury, which also provides a small staff to act as the Club's secretariat. Generally, Paris Club meetings are attended by observers from the IMF, the World Bank, OECD and UNCTAD.

The Club has no funds or resources of its own to lend. Instead, it gives creditor governments an ideal opportunity to discuss international financial problems and to hammer out a common line when negotiating rescheduling deals with debtor nations.

While no formal rules govern the operations of the Paris Club – each request for negotiation is assessed individually – certain basic features have emerged over the years. The creditor countries take a common approach to requests for the renegotiation, thus assuring consistency in treatment of similar types of debt. The Club has drawn a clear distinction for instance, between debt renegotiations to alleviate debt-servicing difficulties and relieve pressure on the balance of payments, and official development assistance.

At the meetings, the debtor country begins with a detailed report on its economic situation and an assessment of the amount and nature of debt relief that it regards as necessary. The IMF representative presents an assessment of the country's economic – especially balance of payments – situation and prospects, including the status of the country's relations with the Fund. The Bank representative then provides a longer-term analysis of the debtor's economic prospects. After statements by UNCTAD and other participants, the creditors' representatives reach an understanding on the general terms of a rescheduling of the country's debt. These become the subject of negotiation between them and the debtor country.

The Paris Club meets normally for two days on a single rescheduling and the results are embodied in a set of Agreed Minutes. These minutes establish the general guidelines for the rescheduling in question and serve as the basis for subsequent bilateral agreements between each creditor and the debtor country. These agreements also cover the interest rate that will apply to the rescheduled debt. A renegotiation achieves legal status only when these bilateral agreements have been reached.

Agreements reached through Paris Club rescheduling deliberations normally:

- only involve loans granted or guaranteed by official agencies of participating creditor countries;
- exclude short-term debt or debts that have been rescheduled before (although there have been exceptions in special circumstances);
- cover payments in arrears, if any, and those falling due in a specified twelve month period and, in some cases, longer;
- reschedule 85-90% of the debt falling due in the specified period

and allow for a grace period of up to five years, with repayments in a further period of up to five years: the non-scheduled portion is generally to be repaid during the grace period;
- request that the debtor should not accord more favoured treatment to debt rescheduled outside the Paris Club and seek to renegotiate other debt on comparable terms;
- require the debtor country, if it is an IMF member, to have in force a stabilization programme with the IMF before rescheduling provisions become effective. Some agreements have extended this requirement to the entire period covered by the rescheduling agreement. Recently, agreements have also stipulated that further rescheduling would only be considered if the country has a programme with the IMF in place.

COMMERCIAL BANK DEBT RESCHEDULING

Commercial bank debt

Commercial bank lending, as already discussed, has become an important source of external finance for many developing countries. With the mounting balance of payments difficulties of countries in recent years, there has been a concomitant increase in the number and scope of restructuring and rescheduling arrangements involving commercial banks. At least twenty-four cases of debt restructuring were completed over 1978-1982, involving fourteen countries (again, as with official reschedulings, some more than once).

Unlike the renegotiation of official debts commercial banks do not have a framework comparable to the Paris Club, although there do exist certain modalities and procedures for negotiations between bankers and their debtor countries. Creditor banks have *ad hoc* arrangements for each rescheduling exercise often involving anywhere up to 1,200 banks from different countries with several lead banks (often the major lenders) guiding the negotiation process. One other difference between commercial bank and Paris Club agreements relates to implementation. Paris Club agreements are arrived at relatively quickly but are implemented over a period of time as the separate bilateral agreements are signed. Commercial bank agreements sometimes take a long time to negotiate but may be implemented fairly rapidly once the basic conditions are met.

Since it is virtually impossible to get representatives of all creditor banks into the negotiations at one time, steering or negotiating committees, often representing national groups of creditor banks are formed to negotiate with the debtor country. On its part, the debtor country may hire investment firms either to advise it during their negotiations or conduct the negotiations on its behalf. The actual negotiations can take place anywhere, and the process can be protracted. In the case of Costa Rica, for example, it took twenty months of sporadic activity to reach agreement.

Most commercial rescheduling arrangements cover medium-term liabilities of the public sector in the debtor countries not covered by official guarantees in the creditor banks' home countries. In some cases the negotiations also encompass long-term debt, either through rescheduling or by rolling over earlier obligations. In other cases, the arrangements seek to restructure arrears on debt-service obligations.

There are two basic principles that underlie commercial bank rescheduling.

A common approach

Firstly, the group of creditor banks agrees to adopt a common approach, that is if any of the banks in the creditors' group breaks the terms of the agreement by attempting to seek bilateral restitution of its loans, often by virtue of a cross default clause, other banks are not bound to conform to the common agreement reached with the debtor country.

Interest payments continue

Secondly (with some exceptions), commercial banks' payment of interest must continue, even while the principal debt is being restructured. In general, interest arrears must be cleared before the rescheduling agreement is signed.

The terms of commercial bank rescheduling vary considerably. Broadly, they include:

- loans falling due over the next one to two years, with a shorter moratorium on arrears;

- 80% (though in some cases less) of the debt due during the consolidation period and in some cases the entire amount;
- interest rates linked to the three or six month London interbank rate for the US dollar or the US prime rate (in the case of dollar denominated debt);
- a refinancing or rescheduling fee of varying amounts;
- and, since 1978, banks almost always require the debtor countries to have an adjustment programme with the Fund before negotiations begin, or before the end of the consolidation period.

Forced rescheduling is a traumatic experience for a country. The period of discussion is long. Therefore, for a long period, the conduct of international trade is limited as banks hesitate in confirming payments to both exporters and importers without sufficient collateral security. Exports are affected as well as imports because banks are reluctant to provide guarantees for contracts (such as bid and performance bonds). The speed at which economic chaos ensues is remarkable and its social and political consequences are enormous. In addition, the direct financial costs of rescheduling are substantial including larger interest payments, various restructuring, legal and accounting fees and considerable out-of-pocket expenses associated with the meetings and negotiations. Perhaps the only positive aspect of rescheduling and financial crisis is the educational aspect. More often than not it takes a crisis to provide support to those groups within ruling bodies which put priority on pragmatism and efficiency in economic management instead of on ideology and local politics. It takes a crisis for both banks and governments to appreciate the depth of the relationship between finance, economics, and politics.

The cost of rescheduling to banks is also considerable. Firstly, it disrupts the flow of funds. Secondly, it hampers a bank's ability to select loans on the basis of profitability and risk. Thirdly, the cost of management time – including senior management, country desk officers, credit officers, lawyers, economists and liability managers – is substantial, to which need to be added costs of communication and travel. A fourth costly aspect is the need for increased reserves against loan losses. All of these constitute direct and opportunity costs. Fifthly, unfavourable publicity affects the price of bank shares and consequently sources of funding and overall lending ability. Nevertheless, if over a period of time the problem is resolved and no write-offs occur, interest and fee earnings from rescheduled amounts reasonably compensate the costs and efforts associated with it.

The increase in the occurrence of reschedulings has a negative effect on international trade. Large amounts of funds which would normally be used to finance trade are not returned to banks for that use and are instead tied up in long-term rescheduling. The general uncertainty in the financial markets causes banks and exporters to be very cautious and selective in accepting additional risks. A large number of small banks and even larger banks have withdrawn from, or limited, international lending. Banks and exporters call on official export guarantees on unpaid loans to problem countries, thereby reducing funds in government export promotion programmes. This is a point which should be borne in mind when analyzing the improved trade surpluses of CMEA. Such achievements may be owing less to improved export performance, or increased administrative control over imports, as to the fact that the sources for financing such imports have become considerably tightened. Combined with the increasing protectionist pressures, prospects for international trade are affected and the nature of international finance altered.

Official and bank rescheduling: recent developments

The incidence of debt defaults and reschedulings until 1981 was low. From 1956 to 1973, ten LDCs[9] – renegotiated debts of around $7 billion in 24 cases of rescheduling and from 1974 to 1979, ten LDCs renegotiated debts of some $10 billion in 16 cases of reschedulings.[10] In 1980, six LDCs renegotiated $4.5 billion of debts, of which $3 billion was accounted for by Turkey alone.

From 1980 to 1984, debt rescheduling became big business. In 1981, fourteen LDCs renegotiated debts of nearly $11 billion and in 1982-1983, over thirty LDCs were involved in the rescheduling of over $100 billion of foreign debt. During this latter period, about half the countries involved in Latin America and Eastern

[9] Argentina, Turkey, Brazil, Chile, Indonesia, Ghana, Peru, India, Pakistan, Cambodia.
[10] Pakistan, Chile, India, Ghana, Zaire, Sierra Leone, Turkey, Peru, Sudan, Togo.

Europe unilaterally ceased payment on all or part of their sovereign debt-service obligations. Unlike previous debt-service interruptions in history, creditor governments were not exposed seriously to debt that could not be serviced. In any case, to the extent that governments might lose financially from debt default or repudiation, losses could be absorbed or made good by the taxpayer. Private commercial banks, on the other hand, were heavily exposed. The risks were not only to the financial standing of individual banks but, through a possible collapse of confidence and a chain reaction of bank failures stopped only by substantial central bank intervention, to the entire global financial system. Furthermore, banks had no gunboats and no means of enforcing the rules of the game other than their legal loan agreements, which were in any event of dubious value.

As a result, banks have had to make concessions in their negotiating positions and yield to demands for lower spreads and fees on new and rescheduled loans. Commercial banks, encouraged by central banks, have approached debt reschedulings on a so-called, case-by-case basis, i.e. dealing with each country's reschedulings separately as it arises, taking a country-specific view in each set of debt renegotiations. This is consistent with the philosophy of the IMF and the US government as regards external debt management, which leads to the conclusion that financial adjustment is the key component of financial equilibrium programmes. According to the views of the IMF and central banks, rescheduling, discussed earlier, has its own rules, providing for:

- emergency short-term bilateral assistance, where necessary, in the form of bridging finance from the BIS and/or creditor governments, which are repaid from IMF or new medium- and long-term bank loans as and when they are disbursed;
- agreement between the borrower and the IMF on a programme of economic adjustment, designed to restore balance of payments equilibrium, debt-servicing ability and international borrowing capacity. Drawdowns on IMF loans are conditional on the country's meeting IMF performance criteria;
- the willingness of commercial banks to continue lending and, where necessary, to provide new money, if only to keep interest payments current;
- further increases in funds available for lending by official institutions;
- sustained economic growth and lower interest rates.

These rules need to be considered in greater detail because there are flaws in the way they hang together. There is not too much of a problem in borrowers receiving bridging finance from the BIS or major central banks, provided such loans are repaid promptly and not renewed or rolled over.

Agreement on an IMF programme is the linchpin of the rules. It opens the door to both IMF financing (with conditions) and to the willingness of commercial banks to reschedule and provide new money. If a country cannot agree the terms of an IMF programme or fails consistently to meet performance criteria, it prejudices its access to both further IMF money and, therefore, to commercial bank financing. At the same time, however, IMF money may be contingent on both agreement to an adjustment programme and on the willingness of commercial banks to provide new money. The web of conditions may be shown schematically, as follows:

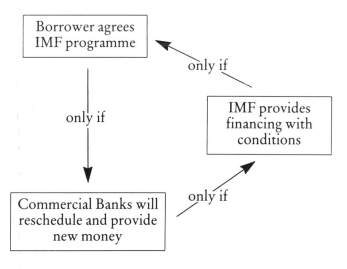

Figure 9.1.

Thus, in some cases, notably those for major borrowers where large amounts of money are involved, it could be argued that no new loans will be forthcoming at all unless an IMF programme is agreed and that, specifically, if commercial banks do not meet their designated share of a country's immediate borrowing needs, no IMF money will be forthcoming, whether or not a programme has been agreed.[11] It is essential, therefore, if reschedulings are to be successful, that the banks and the IMF see their interests as common, for what the preceding arrangements amount to are, in effect, forced or involuntary lending by banks.

In any event, it might be argued that the case-by-case approach advocated by international monetary authorities and preferred by banks is inconsistent with the rules. The rules are, after all, fairly general and in no way country-specific. They do not take account of the social and economic realities in individual debtor countries or the impact of austerity programmes on the well-being of the private sector and on the operation of market mechanisms which are the sacred cows of the IMF and US establishments. Nor do they take account of the impact of austerity in bringing about a sharper pyramidical structure of income distribution in debtor countries where substantial inequalities exist already and which might have adverse political repercussions. Last, but not least, they do not recognize that as each debtor nation implements its austerity programme, a major contradiction is created between countries contracting their economies to achieve balance of payments equilibrium and the needs they all have to develop new goods to sell in new markets.

The irony is that debtor nations, particularly those in Latin America, tend to the view that the debt problem is both general and structural, i.e. the result of depressed export markets and high interest rates and see the solution as global-type initiatives that address those problems. They negotiate their debts and debt obligations, however, with banks, which state the debt problem to be country-specific, do business on the basis of non-specific, generalized rules and yet shy away from any global solutions because of the loss of freedom and flexibility that these would entail. The longer this situation continues, the more likely it is that debtor countries will formulate a common approach to their problems, as they began to do at the Cartagena conference in 1984, and start to demand non-specific terms and conditions in debt negotiations. If and when such a time arises, the opportunities for

---

[11] In the Mexican rescheduling in 1982, IMF Managing Director de Larosiere effectively told the banks that unless they provided $5 billion of Mexico's $8.3 billion borrowing requirement for 1983, he would not recommend acceptance of the Mexican programme by the directors of the IMF. See, Joseph Kraft, *The Mexican Rescue* (Group of Thirty, New York, 1984).

banks to take independent portfolio decisions in which they can assess and price risks and rewards will be limited.

A more pressing reason for debtors' dissatisfaction with the current approach to rescheduling is the persistence of their capital export position, i.e. their new bank loans fall short of their debt-service payments. All that their debt reschedulings are accomplishing are the postponements of the debt-service peaks accompanied by a steady increase in the burden of debt. Thus, for all countries that had rescheduled or were rescheduling at the end of 1983, the improvement in their debt-service situation is short-lived and the problems will resurface in the late 1980s.

Table 9.2. The Postponement of Debt Difficulties
by Rescheduling Efforts to Date*

All Rescheduling Countries	1982	1983	1984	1985	1986	1987	1988
Before Rescheduling ($ billion)							
Principal Payments	32.0	34.6	30.2	31.7	31.6	36.1	42.4
Debt Service Payments	65.5	63.0	58.8	61.8	60.5	65.5	73.3
Debt Service Ratio (%)	45	47	38	37	34	33	35
After Rescheduling ($ billion)							
Principal Payments	20.3	0.8	5.2	33.0	32.7	43.6	60.8
Debt Service Payments	53.8	29.2	33.8	63.1	61.6	73.0	91.7
Debt Service Ratio (%)	37	22	22	38	35	37	44

* It is assumed that interest rates (LIBOR) fall to 7.6% in 1987-1988, that export growth of the LDCs concerned rises by 9.3% p.a. and that economic growth in OECD nations is 2.7% p.a. These assumptions may well be too optimistic, in which case the debt-service burden after 1986 will rise more sharply.

Source: *Royal Bank of Canada*

It is clear that this drawn-out situation is equally disadvantageous in the long-term for both debtor nations and banks aside from the negative consequences on international trade. For debtor nations, the rescheduling discussions are long, complicated and almost an annual event. During these periods, the conduct of international trade is constrained because banks may hesitate to confirm payments to both exporters and importers with sufficient or adequate security. Even export trade may be affected adversely by the reluctance of banks to provide guarantees for contracts, e.g. bid and performance bonds. Aside from these technical costs associated with annual reschedulings, the direct costs are substantial, including larger interest payments, various restructuring, legal and accounting fees and considerable out-of-pocket expenses associated with rescheduling meetings and negotiations. Meanwhile, the real economic issues, as perceived by debtor countries, remain unresolved, or even unattended to.

For banks too the costs, as discussed earlier, are considerable. Rescheduling disrupts the flow of funds into and out of the balance sheet and restricts the bank's ability to make loans on the basis of profitability and risk. The costs of management, including senior management, country lending and credit officers, lawyers, economists, liability managers, communication and travel are substantial, and the reserves held against bad loans or dubious loans disrupt the income statement. All these costs constitute direct and opportunity costs. Finally, adverse publicity regarding bad loans or exposure to major problem debtors affects the bank's share price, its funding capacity and its overall lending ability. Only time – and good fortune – will show whether the interest and fee earnings from rescheduling will compensate for the costs and repercussions associated with it.

As far as international trade is concerned, it is apparent that large volumes of funds which would normally be used to finance trade are not returned to banks for that use. Rather, they are either committed as new money in reschedulings (to pay interest on debt) or they become earmarked for wholly different purposes as banks and exporters reduce their appetite for risk. As stated before, some smaller banks have withdrawn from international lending altogether and medium-sized and large banks here also reduced the scale of their international lending activities. Banks and exporters have recourse to official export guarantees on unpaid trade debts from problem debtors, thereby reducing the funds available in government export promotion programmes. Some such agencies, e.g. The Export Credit Guarantee Department of the UK, have recorded losses for the first time ever and not only curbed the range of activities, or countries against which they will insure, but also increased the costs of insurance premiums. In the final analysis, the tax-payer in creditor nations pays the bill. Constraints on funds available for trade finance from both private and official sources reinforce protectionist tendencies in international trade and render even more difficult the export promotion efforts which debtor nations need so much to realize. It is necessary to reiterate the involuntary nature of debt rescheduling, which contrasts sharply with the free choice which banks exercised when participating initially in syndicated loans.

The demand to renegotiate debt is usually presented by the borrower as a *fait accompli*, whether or not as a result of a unilateral moratorium on debt-service payments. Normally, borrowers have sought quick decisions and required instant ratification of the ensuing transactions by each of the lending institutions involved. In this respect, small banks are at an even bigger disadvantage than large banks. They tend not to have any part in the actual debt renegotiations, nor to have the option to reject the resulting rescheduling package and, in the end, they are required by the large banks on the Steering (rescheduling) Committee to commit funds in an equitable manner, i.e. usually in proportion to their exposure. Some banks, which confined their international lending activities to short-term, self-liquidating trade finance transactions, were suddenly caught up in the rescheduling of medium- and long-term public sector debt over six to eight years. These banks have complained, with some justification, that they only provided finance to cover transactions between their well-known domestic corporate clients and known clients in one or more major debtor nations.

They did not feel obliged to pay for the mistakes of the large banks and were reluctant to contribute to the new money loans that the large banks sought to provide; and some did not contribute. This situation creates problems for the larger banks which, in some cases, might have to increase their own exposure in order to meet the demands by borrowers that short-term credit lines be maintained as part of the rescheduling agreements.

The most sensitive problems of all, however, concerns the provision of new money, as the following data demonstrate:

Table 9.3. International Lending Activity ($ billion)

	1982	1983
Total lending	116.5	96.5
– of which, voluntary to non-LDCs	59.0	29.4
– of which, voluntary to LDCs	32.0	8.6
– of which, involuntary to LDCs	25.5	58.5
– of which, rescheduling	14.3	43.4
– of which, new money	11.2	15.1

Source: *Bank of England Quarterly Bulletin*

By new money is meant the idea of involuntary lending, i.e. an agreement with banks by which each individual bank agrees to increase its exposure by a given percentage, in the framework of an overall agreement often including the IMF. This involuntary lending plus rescheduling rose from just over $25 billion in 1982 to nearly $60 billion in 1983. Whilst this fell a little short of voluntary lending to LDCs in 1982, it was between six and seven times as big in 1983. The effect of this new money involuntary lending is to capitalize interest payments on past debt which may prevent the critical situation of having to declare a borrower in default but which can hardly be deemed to represent sound banking practice, particularly if it is sustained over a long period. In actual fact, this situation can probably not be sustained. It involves borrowers who cannot service their debts, though lenders pretend otherwise and need not, therefore, repudiate them and invite retaliation or punishment from lenders. Lenders do not declare default and do not, therefore, have to punish themselves through writing off the loan(s) involved. However, if the regulatory authorities over banks continue to press for more and higher loan loss provisions, it can only be a question of time before the scale of loan write offs means that some lenders may have to declare a formal default in order to get tax relief on their loan losses. With or without such a development, one would have to question the willingness of banks to continue putting up new money to perpetuate the pretence that interest payments are being, and will continue to be, met.

Banks and major debtors are, therefore, locked into a vicious circle. Debtor nations continue to fail to meet debt-service payments or require new loans for that purpose. Banks have to continue borrowing dollars which ordinarily would have been repaid or borrowing additional sums of money to cover the new money they have to continue to make available to problem countries.

This demand for dollars (on-lent to countries to give them time to adjust to high interest rates and depressed export markets) collides with other demands for credit associated with the US budget deficit and normal private sector borrowing to produce or sustain high interest rates. These, in turn, in conjunction with austerity programmes and restrictive monetary policies reinforce the weaknesses in worldwide demand and limit the upward potential for commodity prices and export earnings.

Thus, high interest rates and slow economic growth are, in the first place, the cause of the global debt problem but, subsequently, the result of it. In other words, the debt problem is tending to sustain its own causes and, ultimately, this must bring the debt players nearer and nearer to actual or *de facto* default, since reschedulings are buying time which cannot effectively be utilized to good effect.

Appendix 9.1

THE PRISONERS' DILEMMA AS APPLIED TO THE DEBT CRISIS

An interesting analysis of the reasons for the plethora of pre-1930 defaults versus the post-1945 rescheduling arrangements has been provided by Sachs[12]. He argues that the early period was characterized by non-co-operative strategies of creditors and debtors, while the post-1945 period is characterized by extensive bargaining and co-operative strategies by banks and the LDCs. Sachs goes on to illustrate how game theory can contribute to this change in behaviour. It is essential to distinguish here between a situation where the players co-operate or do not co-operate.

In the co-operative case, the game theorists have tended to argue that the players will be sufficiently rational to discover and make full use of all opportunities which can be mutually advantageous. That is, the players are taken to co-operate on any and every action which can increase the pay-off of either players (provided it does not, at the same time, reduce the pay-off of the other).

In the non co-operative case both players will often be led by self-interest to take decisions which are mutually disadvantageous. This has been illustrated sharply by a game entitled the "prisoners' dilemma" which is attributed to A.W. Tucker. The dilemma occurs where individuals, or firms, or political parties, or any organized groups, cannot arrange a binding agreement among themselves because they cannot control the other decisions.

The analogy is with prisoners interrogated separately, each of whom knows that if none confesses all will receive a light sentence for want of hard evidence. If one confesses (and the others do not) he will go free and the others will receive harsh sentences; if all

[12] J. Sachs, *LDC Debt in the 1980s. Risks and Reforms*, NBER Working Paper, No. 861 (Feb. 1982).

confess each will receive a sentence less severe than if all but one remained silent, but more severe than if none confessed. If each acts to protect himself he will confess whatever the others do. But what is rational for each one in the absence of agreement nevertheless leads to a situation in which all are worse off than they might have been with agreement.

The co-operative and non co-operative strategies within the international debt game can be illustrated by a pay-off matrix (the first entry in each cell is the creditor pay-off and the second entry the debtor pay-offs). The creditor bank has three possible strategies: reduce loans, maintain loans, or increase loans. The debtor has two possible strategies: restrain demand or default. In the non co-operative strategy, the debtor prefers to default no matter what the strategy pursued by the creditor and the creditor wants to call in the loans no matter what action the debtor takes. The resulting non co-operative solution, the top right hand corner yields (–2, 1) the situation which occurred in the pre-1930s' situation.

Table 9.4. Creditor Strategy/Debtor Strategy

	Restrain Demand	Default
Reduce Loans	2, –1	–2, 1
Maintain Loans	1, 0	–5, 2
Increase Loans	0, 2	–10, 3

Source: Sachs, *op.cit.*

However, if the two parties could co-operate it is possible to have a situation where both parties are better off. If agreement could be reached on an appropriate IMF-monitored austerity programme with debt rescheduling it is possible to move to a situation where one could have increased loans by the creditor and demand restraint by the debtor.

So the bottom left-hand corner situation of (0,2) – the post-1945 situation – is clearly superior for both parties than the previous (–2,1) situation.

Chapter 10

Proposals for Resolving the International Debt Crisis

Solutions for the debt crisis range from doing nothing (i.e. let the free market operate) to a complete restructuring of the international monetary system (*via* Bretton Woods Mark II). Between these two extremes lies a range of alternatives, some dealing with repayment of capital and some repayment of interest. Two broad issues arise in conjunction with the resolution of the international debt problem. Firstly, who bears the losses, if any, arising from the bad debt? And secondly, what reforms are required to reduce the probability of a similar situation arising in the future? Turning to the first issue, there are only three possibilities:

- the debtor countries make the fiscal adjustments and reductions in general expenditure which are required to service their external debt;
- the lending institutions absorb the losses arising from their previous lending decision;
- the losses are shifted, in whole or in part, to a third party, namely the tax-payers of the creditor countries.

Only some combination of the first and second of these meets simple tests of fairness and avoids setting an improper precedent. To be sure, the debtor countries have ample incentive to service their external debt, for the future costs of today's default would indeed be high.

The final solutions should never be contemplated as long as the first and second can be implemented without serious risk of collapse of the international financial system, a risk that can be clearly avoided by orderly liquidation of the insolvent institutions. To permit the final solution would be to invite repetition of the problem and, ultimately, the virtual nationalisation (*via* regulation) of the basic entities of the international financial system.

As the *Amex Bank Review* (June 19, 1984) stresses, the various schemes designed to resolve the second broad issue aim at one or more of the following results:

- giving banks more secure assets in place of existing LDC loans;
- giving banks time to write down loans;
- reducing the LDCs' current debt-service burden by forgiving or delaying current interest payments;
- reducing the overall burden of LDC debts by forcing banks to take a loss, usually in return for a guarantee;
- encouraging new lending to LDCs.

A number of proposals for dealing with the problem have been discussed. Two of these – some form of asset sales and new procedures or institutions – are discussed in detail. Other schemes – interest rate capping reduction of US interest rates *etc.*, will be discussed below.

Free market solution

Many US academics, most notably Dr Brunner (known in the UK as the man who is reputed to have converted Mrs Thatcher to monetarism), argue that the crisis should be resolved through the interplay of free market forces, that commercial banks should write off their existing loans to hard-pressed debtor-countries over an extended period if necessary and should provide fresh credit to LDC borrowers only on the basis of their own commercial judgement.

This view has found little favour in US banking circles (the US commercial banks being relatively heavily committed to problem-borrowers) but has been more warmly received in Continental Europe where many banks are less heavily exposed to LDC problem loans.

The great fear with this view is that, as the international banks are heavily interlinked through the medium of the interbank market, a single large default could bring down the whole system and lead to a breakdown in trade and to 1930s' type world depression.

Case by case approach

The current scheme for solving the problem can be summarized by the term *case by case approach*. What this means is that individual defaulting countries are judged on their merit and, if they accept and implement IMF austerity packages that the terms of the loans become less onerous.

Support for the case by case approach comes from the results of a computer-based model for the nineteen largest debtor countries, undertaken by William Cline. Relating their exports to OECD growth, imports to domestic growth, both to the exchange rate and taking account of interest rates, oil prices, and dollar strength, Cline finds that if OECD growth reaches an average of 3% in 1984-1986 (a feasible goal in view of past recovery experience), the debt burden should decline. The external deficit falls from 24 to 14% of exports and the ratio of debt to exports from 190 to 160%. The improvement is greater for oil importers and less for oil exporters. The key debtors – Brazil, Mexico and Argentina – all show substantial improvement. The broad conclusion is that the debt problem is one of temporary liquidity, not fundamental insolvency.

However, the prognosis depends on successful OECD recovery. At 2% growth or below, the debt problem worsens. It is also necessary to avoid stratospheric interest rates, increased trade protection and either a collapse or another explosion in the price of oil.

Morgan Guaranty (World Financial Markets, June 1983), also provide support for this view. Their base case consists of six assumptions:

- a moderate OECD recovery that begins in 1983 and gathers strength in 1984-1985, averaging 3% *per annum* with 3% *per annum* growth thereafter;
- industrial country inflation, as measured by wholesale manufacturers' prices in local currency terms, that rises gradually from an average of 4% in 1983 to 6% *per annum* in 1985 and thereafter;
- some softening of the dollar in 1983 and continuing into 1984-1985 but which still leaves the dollar about 10% above its 1975-1979 average on a real effective basis;
- interest rates, as represented by LIBOR for six month

Eurodollars that decline to an average of 8% in 1984 and to average 9%, or 3% in real terms in the second half of the 1980s;

- oil prices, as measured by the effective average OPEC price, that average $28 *per* barrel in 1983, rise to $32 by 1985 and remain constant in real terms thereafter;
- prices of non-oil commodities, as measured by a composite dollar index, that increase by about 25% between 1982 and 1985.

Under these conditions, it is estimated that exports of goods and services of the twenty-one major LDC borrowers would grow at an average rate of 11% *per annum* in this decade. In relation to exports of goods and services, the current account deficit would fall sharply, and continue declining to about 5% in the latter part of this decade. Total external debt in relation to exports however, would fall more gradually, from nearly 180% in 1982 to about 165% in 1985 and about 125% by 1990.

The overall results for major LDC borrowers are quite sensitive to changes in key assumptions about world economic conditions from those used in the base case. The greatest sensitivity is to the OECD growth rate, where a 1% change from the base case beginning in 1984 can affect the current account balance by about $11 billion (or 3% of exports) in 1985 and approximately $85 billion (14% of exports) by 1990. The debt/export ratio would scarcely improve during the remainder of the decade if the OECD growth rate were 1% lower than in the base case. The results are also very sensitive to a 1% per annum change in the terms of trade after 1983, particularly as the effects accumulate through the remainder of the decade.

The IMF, as already indicated, does not support any of the generalized schemes discussed below for solving the debt-problems. Their support for the case by case approach is based on three propositions. Firstly, it argues that the circumstances of individual debtors are highly varied, in terms of the size of their economic adjustment needs, their capacity to adjust and the features of their external debt. Thus, the right solution for one country may be no solution at all for another. Secondly, it argues that there is the need for equity among debtors and among creditors and also that there is the question of incentives and disincentives. The case by case approach permits a keener focus on the needs and responsibilities of each debtor country and creditor institution. Finally, it suggests that while it seems unlikely that public funds could be mobilized on the scale required for any sweeping attack on the debt problem in general, it has proved possible to attract the financial support of certain governments and central banks for individual debtor countries.

It must be remembered that the continued lending by commercial banks, essential under the case by case approach, is basically imprudent. Banks continue to do so since it may often be the core of a rescheduling deal but, in any event, it avoids having to declare a borrower in default and is necessary simply to keep the existing situation from deteriorating. The banks are, therefore, protecting their exposure by increasing it and this is clearly unsustainable.

What the case by case approach lacks, however, is a strategic approach to the restoration of financial strength and borrowing capacity. This can only come about if banks are prepared to stretch out the terms of rescheduled debt say, over fifteen to twenty-five years with a four to five year grace period and with repayment obligations tailored to the cash-flow generating capacity of the country. There is little, if anything, to be gained by any of the players from the universal application of standard, short-term rescheduling terms and conditions.

Alternative international debt solution proposals can be divided into those which affect the principal outstanding and those which seek to affect the interest burden.

Proposals which affect the principal outstanding

Nearly all the proposals in this category have a common element, namely some type of bailout of the international commercial banks. Most of the proposals involve the creation of new funds (or guarantees) through national or international institutions – the national central banks, the IMF, the BIS, or the World Bank – to secure the loans previously made to the developing countries.

The call in many quarters is for a new Bretton Woods (named after the conference which originally set up the IMF). The conference would seek to formalize, through international agreement, the arrangements which have evolved since the Mexican moratorium, thereby providing the assurance of a credit flow, on IMF terms, to debtor-countries in a scale large enough to ward off the threat of default.

Such a measure is objectionable on at least two grounds. Firstly, an increase in IMF resources would very likely imply a commensurate increase in world liquidity and hence inflation. Secondly, it constitutes a step in the direction of rewarding bank mismanagement (the moral hazard problem discussed in chapter 7) and postponing adjustment by financing disequilibrium situations.

Many plans for repaying the principal have been put forward. Those propounded by Rohatyn, Kenen, Mackworth-Young, Bailey, Leslie, Meier-Preschany, Yassukovitch and Wallich are discussed below.

The Rohatyn plan

Probably the best-known proposal for a world discount house that would relieve commercial banks of problem sovereign debt comes from Lazard Freres & Co. partner Felix Rohatyn, who masterminded New York City's bailout in the mid-1970s. As in most schemes, the banks' old loans would be swapped for guaranteed, tradeable paper – in this case, for long-term, low interest bonds, issued by an IMF or World Bank affiliate or other agency, which would in turn supply massive debt relief to the LDCs.

Rohatyn notes that if, say, $300 billion in short-term credits was stretched out twenty-five to thirty years at an average 6% interest rate (about half the going rate for LDCs), the annual interest savings would be $15 billion to $20 billion. Moreover, he believes his scheme "will make it more likely" that the banks will lend the additional money LDCs need to boost exports since, although they will lose current cash flow, they will be upgrading asset quality. "Guaranteed flows at 6% may be worth more than non-guaranteed flows at 13%", he suggests.[1]

The agency could help debtor nations establish revenue streams tied to exports that would be used to service the bonds. Bank losses incurred either through such comprehensive rescheduling or from external write offs may leave lenders with insufficient capital, requiring central banks to become investors of last resort.

The New York City rescue involved the establishment by the Federal Government of an agency, the Municipal Assistance Corporation (MAC), to administer the city's finances. Coupon

---

[1] Testimony by Felix Rohatyn before the Committee on Foreign Relations, US Senate, Washington, (17 Jan, 1983).

reductions and a substantial lengthening of the average maturity of outstanding New York City debt were agreed by creditors in exchange for the acceptance by the city authorities of stringent MAC-supervised budgetary policies. The proposal now is that a similar solution to that which was implemented in the New York City crisis should be applied to those sovereign borrowers who currently face difficulties in servicing their debts.

There is, however, at least one crucial difference between the circumstances of the New York City crisis and present international debt problems. The difference is that there was a superior legal and administrative authority, namely, the US Federal Government, to arrange, and give its backing to the New York City rescue, whereas the supra-national authority required to support an assistance corporation operating on an international scale does not, as yet, exist. Debtor governments might agree to budgetary restraint but, in the event, renege on their undertakings without there being any authority in a position to enforce sanctions. In practice, with both debtors and creditors aware of the assistance corporation's lack of effective sanctions, debtor governments would probably be able to drive a hard bargain with their creditors, with the cost being borne primarily by bank shareholders or taxpayers in the industrial countries.

The major difficulty with the Rohatyn scheme is that it does involve losses for banks while still leaving assets frozen until a reasonable secondary market is established.

Kenen plan

Princeton University professor Peter Kenen proposes for more modest debt relief and pays more attention to creating a workable secondary market. His International Debt Discount Corporation (IDDC), is designed to make a "once only" offer to the bank for their LDC loans at 10% discount. In the interests of consistency and to create a standard trading instrument, the IDCC would publish standard terms for doing business with debtors. It would extend maturities and use five of the ten cents on the dollar extracted from banks for debt relief.

The IDCC's terms appear generous to the banks, yet Kenen would discourage bankers from using the discount facility as a trash heap for, say, Polish or Sudanese paper. Any bank could tender, as a possible figure, 60% of qualifying assets – but only on a *pro rata* basis. He insists that the banks can't have an open-ended option to dump their worst assets.

So the IDDC would exchange bonds for developing country loans, discounted according to their relative riskiness. Only loans to those countries with IMF programmes and which recognize the corporation as successor claimant to the banks would be eligible. Earnings from discounting could provide debt relief. Geoffrey Bell, a director of Schroder International, expressed a general criticism of the Kenen/Rohatyn model arguing that the schemes don't address themselves to the real issue, namely how to get real money to these countries, rather than dealing with existing debts. (Bell has himself proposed an international lending facility, linked to the IMF: banks would place funds in the facility which the IMF would lend alongside its own loans). Rohatyn and Kenen assume new lending to LDCs on a normal commercial basis. But Mackworth-Young's idea (discussed below) tackles Bell's criticism.

Mackworth-Young plan

The plan of the late Morgan Grenfell & Co. chairman, G.W. Mackworth-Young has two stages. In the first, as an interim measure, the banks would surrender, at full value, their locked-in loans to some arm of the BIS, the IMF, or a new agency in exchange for non interest-bearing bonds. This would free them of the need to fund the debts. Later, in the second stage, these bonds would be convertible into guaranteed quadruple-A-rated bonds bearing interest, which would be tradeable on a secondary market, but on conversion the banks would mark their securities to market (i.e. value them at the going market rate). The two stage approach allows the banks to defer any write-down until their capital ratios permit.

The same sort of limitations as were suggested for the Rohatyn plan are true for those of Kenen and Mackworth-Young.

Bailey plan

Norman Bailey, a senior director of the US National Security Council, would rather rely on the free market to create liquidity for the banks. He proposes that banks continue to receive interest on their loans so that they will not have to write down their assets (as they must if they receive lower-than-market interest rates). But in place of principal repayments, debtors would issue an indexed contract called an "exchange participation note" guaranteeing the banks a fixed percentage of their foreign exchange receipts. These certificates would be fully negotiable. This proposal does attempt to gear rescue plans to the LDCs' ability to pay, but again it would cut bank earnings. Controversy also surrounds how one would measure "ability to pay".

The Leslie plan

Peter Leslie, Senior General Manager at Barclays Bank International, gives support for a rediscount solution. A rediscount facility, he argues, would enable the commercial banks to mobilize a part of their medium-term debt, which has arisen as a result of rescheduling, with their central bank or other appropriate body on the basis that the proceeds were used to create fresh lendings. The rediscounted debts would come off the balance sheet of the commercial bank and thus no longer require appropriate liquidity and prudential capital support. They would possibly still need to be treated as contingent liabilities since, if the debt was unpaid, then a write-off would ultimately have to take place in the books of the commercial bank as the original lender. The rediscount would cover the full length of the maturity and appropriate arrangements would have to be made covering the interest factor.

It's quite interesting to note that, since January 1984, foreign banks in Brazil have been selling Brazilian loans on their books at a discount under an agreement worked out by Brazil and these creditors banks. Sale of the loans reduces the banks' concern regarding participating in the next phase of loan renegotiations. Companies which have been buying the 10 to 30% discounted loans enjoy tax and accounting advantages while the Brazilian government has its external debt lowered. However, as of June 13, 1984, the Brazilian central bank suspended this arrangement, fearing that the increasing discounting would bring about a loss of confidence.

Meier-Preschany plan

Manfred Meier-Preschany, who is a member of the managing board of Dresdner Bank, has put forward a similar proposal: the world bank rather than central banks would take problem debts off the banks' balance sheets, while the banks retain the risk. The debts should be converted into long-term loans or bonds.

Yassukovitch plan

Stanilas Yassukovitch of Merrill Lynch has suggested that all loans recently negotiated between banks and troubled debtors should be converted into IMF facilities and IMF should replace the lead banks as agents – so commercial banks are removed from direct involvement in adjustment programmes. Bank exposure should then be redistributed over twenty years to a consortium of central banks and export credit agencies in industrial countries, regional development banks, the IMF and the World Bank.

The common feature of these plans is the removal of bad debts from the balance sheets of the lending banks so as to stabilize their position and provide them indirectly with new liquidity. The idea is that these debts would be bought back at a price less than their nominal value (a discount of 10% to 15% for instance) either by some newly created agency, for example, some international debt retirement fund, or by the IMF (or the central banks according to some versions), or even by investment mechanisms on some secondary market (to be set up for the purpose).

The authors of these plans believe they have two virtues: firstly, they make it possible to restore a certain truthfulness to balance sheets and secondly, they also improve bank liquidity at the cost of limited accounting losses. Moreover, consolidating these debts over a very long time period (up to thirty years) and with a very low interest rate, would reduce the borrowers' debt servicing costs.

However, as Laulan has pointed out, these plans have serious flaws. They are dangerous in the short run in as much as they would be likely to precipitate the very crisis they aim to avert. They are counter-productive inasmuch as the long-term side effects, even assuming an immediate crisis is avoided, would make the cure worse than the disease. Implementing them would be very likely to damage the reputation of the lending institutions, whose real or supposed management errors would thereby be revealed in broad daylight, and at the same time ruin the credit of the debtors whose solvency troubles would be cruelly brought to the fore. If such plans were applied, they would undoubtedly help to make the loans granted to the Third World in the 1970s go down in history alongside the notorious Russian loans.

What is wrong with asset sales?

Expressed more systematically, the main objections to all these plans may be summarized as follows:

- It is doubtful under present circumstances that institutions or individuals operating on a secondary market would be inclined to buy bad debts with just 10% discount. A discount of 50% or more would seem more likely. That would be enough to cast a shadow over the reputation of the debtor nations and cause the creditor banks to withdraw permanently from this kind of operation.
- The possibility of having the IMF or some other financial institution buy these debts with a reasonable discount, raises objections of another kind. One can well imagine the difficulties involved in defining which bad debts are eligible. Even if this delicate issue were resolved, an opportunity of this kind would bring about a vast shift in debt positions, on the part of small US banks and by the larger banks under pressure from their shareholders. Indeed, they would be sorely tempted to unload much of their third world portfolios in the rediscount institution.

One step removed from the above asset-sale ideas are the plans to offer guarantees for bank lending. Again, several variants are discussed below.

The Wallich plan

One of the most controversial of the plans to encourage banks to extend new international credits to developing countries has been put forward by Henry Wallich, a member of the Board of Governors of the US Federal Reserve System.[2] This plan entails the creation of a bank lending insurance fund.

Wallich stresses the two options, insurance of specific loans and

[2] *Insurance of Bank Lending to Developing Countries*, (Group of Thirty, May 1984).

insurance of loan portfolios of banks. Wallich regards insurance of specific loans as too cumbersome to implement and as subject to a number of problems that might hinder its efficiency. One of the major problems with insurance of specific loans, warns Wallich, is that of moral hazard, whereby once a loan contract has been executed, "borrowers might subsequently engage in policies that would inappropriately increase risk".[3] He also argues that specific loan insurance would promote less-efficient resource allocations as well as discrimination against the more creditworthy borrowers should the premiums charged for insurance not include adequate differentials to reflect differences in risk among borrowers.

The most viable technique, in Wallich's view, would be the insuring of some fraction of banks' portfolios of loans to developing countries. He estimates that 2% would be sufficient to permit a considerable margin of safety for banks, taking into account historical trends in the loss-loan ratios of their international assets. Under this approach, any loan in trouble would be guaranteed by the insurance fund, provided that the overall share of troubled loans in a bank's portfolio did not exceed the insured fraction. This technique would not only help to avoid some of the problems inherent in insuring specific loans, he maintains, but would at the same time encourage bank prudence, since only a portion of banks' portfolios would be insured.

Mr. Wallich suggests that the insurance fund could be designed to guarantee payments of principal, interest, or a combination of the two. He contends that insurance of interest income is the more viable alternative, since a loss of such income could do more immediate damage to a bank's assets than would an eventual loss of principal. He adds that the latter could be "stretched out by rescheduling so long as interest is paid through insurance or perhaps new loans".[4] Furthermore, Mr. Wallich points out, if payment of principal were to be guaranteed, the amounts to be insured would be large and would thus require that the fraction of total loans covered be small, relative to the coverage that could be obtained if only payments of interest were to be guaranteed.

The effectiveness of an insurance fund will depend, to a large extent, on its level of resources. For this reason, Mr. Wallich reasons that the average flows of receipts not only must be

---

[3] *IMF Survey* (Oct. 1983).
[4] *Ibid.*

sufficient to cover regular outflows but also must provide a level of reserves that will generate confidence in the ability of the fund to meet occasional large losses. Mr. Wallich observes that many individual banks are already practising self-insurance, setting aside part of their earnings to cover eventual regular losses. Although pooling these funds would be beneficial in that it would help to spread the risk, the total level of resources might not be sufficient to insure banks against a period of high losses, Mr. Wallich warns. Additional contributions by banks would therefore be needed. These could be financed either by imposing surcharges on loans or by channelling to the insurance pool some of the earnings from the large spreads that banks have been charging for debt rescheduling operations. But, even taking into account these additional contributions, he cautions, the insurance fund might require outside sources of funds. In Mr. Wallich's view, these external sources of funds should take the form of revolving credit facilities to be repaid over time. They would be provided by governments, by international organisations, or by private insurance companies. If funds from governments are used, Mr. Wallich points out, these conceivably could be provided by existing official agencies with insurance or guarantee powers. He explains that, while such guarantees would absorb funds that otherwise could be used to finance other developing country credit, use in an insurance plan for commercial bank loans that insured only a fraction of the portfolio would have higher leverage and could thus promote a relatively larger level of loans.

Implications of the Wallich plan

The type of plan described raises many questions, Mr. Wallich notes. Included among them are the following: who will have overall responsibility for the smooth functioning of the plan? To what degree would banks and borrowers participate on a voluntary basis? And what would be their attitudes to the plan? In addition, Mr. Wallich warns, the plan could give rise to a number of broader economic issues that would need to be addressed. An insurance plan might "reduce the discipline of the markets", might lead to subsidization of weak participants by strong ones – or of private interests by the public – or it might be viewed as a bailout for banks. He contends, however, that "these dangers seem avoidable, through the proper structuring of the plan, through charging of differential rates and, in general, by taking these concerns into account in the design and the administration of the plan".[5]

Zombanakis[6]

Mr. Minos Zombanakis, suggests that all the twenty-five or so countries rescheduling their debts should make thirteen-year agreements with the IMF. Normal commercial bank lending to these countries could then resume, for projects that accorded with their new IMF agreements, provided the IMF was enabled to make one guarantee namely, that if a borrower had fulfilled all the IMF conditions for ten years and had still failed to repay its debts – which should be rare because of the scope for improvement in most of their present policies – then the IMF itself would guarantee the repayments of the debts in years eleven to thirteen.

So a facility would be set up and administered by the IMF in conjunction with the programme of adjustment. It could be called a Guaranteed Loan Fund. Zombanakis claims several benefits for his proposals:

- they do not require the banks to be bailed out, nor do they let the banks off the hook;
- they allow lenders and creditors time to make a realistic adjustment to a deep-rooted problem that cannot be handled through short-term programmes and reschedulings;
- developing countries are spared programmes of extreme devaluation that expose them to the dangers of political upheaval, damaging both to their own constituency and also to their region;
- by rescheduling short-term assets and adding the IMF's guarantee, the banks can foresee their assets and resume their function of financing trade and investment with renewed confidence.
- the banks would no longer have to charge exorbitant rates to good customers in order to create the excess pool of profit required to be able to write off the losses inherent in developing countries loans;
- there would be no interruption of the present *modus operandi* of the financial system. The interbank market would not be at risk;

[5] *Ibid.*
[6] *The Economist* (30 April, 1983).

- the Group of Ten countries, which will have to carry the burden of rescuing the world if there is a debt repudiation, can look forward to thirteen years of breathing space for the LCD's to adjust their economies;
- with the right policies of growth by the industrialized countries and co-operation between the IMF, the banks and the borrowers, the guarantees would never have to be called upon.

There are two major flaws with the Zombanakis plan. Firstly, there is no guarantee that the debtor nations will play by the rules. There is no guarantee that some of these countries, if allowed to borrow large sums for ". . . projects that accorded with their new IMF agreements . . ." would indeed spend all the borrowed money on the designated projects. In many of the indebted countries there is a well-documented history of diversion of funds borrowed for projects to other uses: military, infrastructure building, subsidizing of food destined for their urban populations, servicing of previous loans and enrichment of political leaders and their entourages. Secondly, as discussed earlier, the external debt problem of some Latin American economies derives not only from macroeconomic maladjustment but also from an internal debt problem. More specifically, individual companies (both private and public) have succeeded in borrowing well in excess of the amounts needed for normal fixed and working capital financing (e.g. to finance operating losses and financial charges). Domestic banks as well as the external banks have sustained these excesses in borrowing.

Lever plan

Lord Lever, formally Financial Secretary to the UK Treasury and a leading member of the Labour Cabinet during the period following the first oil crisis, suggests that export credit agencies of the industrialized countries create a central agency which would maintain a measured flow of funds to the developing countries. On the basis of the IMF advice, the agency would notify central banks of developing countries, that individual export credit agencies would ensure bank lending to cover a given current-account deficit.

Lever is anxious to stress that the interest component of the debts are paid, since if interest is not paid, then the loans become non-performing and confidence in banks would be violently shaken. He stresses that the major governments should step in with some collective government support scheme which would enable these debtor countries to meet their interest payments, or else have them met under surveillance by a fund created by the participating governments for the purpose. Otherwise there would be no further mileage in the banks continuing to pretend that their loans are performing when they aren't: this will simply erode confidence even further. Once interest is clearly being remitted, it then becomes possible to contemplate the banks writing down the principal over a period of many years. The attraction of the Lever scheme is its close link with international trade promotion. The problem would be in deciding who should fund the agency.

The Bolin plan

William Bolin, vice chairman of Bank of America, suggests the creation of an Export Development Fund. Backed by the export credit agencies of the industrialized countries and allied with the World Bank, it would make loans beyond the optimum maturities for private banks (seven to eight years) and less than the fifteen year or longer maturities that make best use of World Bank funds. It would fund itself by placing its own floating rate and eight to fourteen year notes with Euromarket investors. The Export Development fund might also participate with commercial and development banks in larger project loans, carrying the middle maturities.

Laulan plan

Yves Laulan,[7] whilst working as group economic advisor to Société Générale argued that the real problem is not so much to deal with the outstanding debt as to give priority to new debt. For such a process to occur, it is necessary to re-establish confidence at two levels. Firstly, a way must be found to make sure that in future the best possible use is made of the funds made available to borrowing countries. The current crises, he claims, is to a large extent due to poor resource allocation. Far more credit was granted than was reasonable over and beyond the moral absorbtive

[7] *The Banker* (June 1983).

capacity of the borrowing nations. Secondly, he argues, bankers must be able to recover their confidence in reasonable operations in the third world so that they do not give in to a panic reaction of mere distrust as far as this kind of operation is concerned.

On the basis of this sort of reasoning, Laulan goes on to argue that it is possible to envisage "upstream" and "downstream" solutions for bank loans. The purpose of both would be to reorganize the relationships between the leading international banks, the IMF and the World Bank.

Upstream

Banks should promise to provide systematic information about their intentions to grant loans to any borrowing nation, to be sent to the IMF for general loans and to the World Bank for project financing. There would thus be a systematic form of consultation and analysis before the loans were made. That would put an end to "telex lending" which has contributed considerably to increasing indebtedness. Banks, he argues, cannot carry out such prior studies because they lack the technical facilities to do so. But the IMF and the World Bank have well-staffed technical departments capable of providing this service. That will not be easy to achieve. The Fund and World Bank people like to keep secrets and they are wary of banks. They will not open up their files willingly but, over time, their distrust may be overcome.

Downstream

In return for this prior examination, the commercial banks might be given a guarantee of some sort. Their main concern nowadays, Laulan believes, is to get their money back. They do not always succeed in doing so. The present spate of rescheduling arrangements, even if the result does not immediately show up as losses on bank balance sheets, entails a serious future threat for the banks' operating accounts and they are aware of that. So their chief concern today is security rather than a return on investment. That is why the intervention of the Fund and World Bank could prove valuable. Banks must have more confidence if they are to continue to engage in an adequate amount of lending. They must be sure that, under certain conditions, part of the risks involved will be borne by some international insurance system, comprised of a network of international institutions. Laulan's proposals raise legal and confidentiality problems, but they have the merit of working within the existing framework of relationships between the multilateral institutions and commercial banks.

The Meltzer plan

The usual way of dealing with debtors who cannot pay their debts is to sell their property and settle their debts. This traditional practice has not been used with international loans because many of the loans are guaranteed by sovereign governments. These guarantees have been debased, however, as discussed in chapter 6, by the policies many of these governments followed. Instead of encouraging efficiency and growth, many of the debtor countries followed inflationary policies, built large central government bureaucracies and allowed them to control most of the investment and a large share of the spending financed by foreign loans.

The governments in the debtor countries now own or control many firms and valuable assets, including oil wells, petrochemical plants and banks in Mexico, iron ore, electric power plants and petroleum refineries in Brazil and other assets elsewhere. These government corporations can be a source of profits if they are operated efficiently. They also offer a way to reduce the external debt to manageable size.

Professor Alan Meltzer has suggested that the debtor countries should exchange part of the outstanding debt for equity shares that the government control. The exchange would lighten their debt burden and improve the quality of the banks' claims. The debtors would, of course, have to make the politically difficult decision to surrender partial control of state-owned enterprises. But, Meltzer argues, this could be less costly than the most likely alternatives – continued severe reductions in standards of living for most of the population, or an explicit moratorium on debt payments.

In March 1985, Mexico announced that it was proposing letting foreign banks swap some of their loans to Mexican government companies for partial ownership in key government enterprises. Some creditor banks received a draft list of nearly 40 companies being considered for debt to equity swaps, including some strategic state-owned enterprises that produce steel, trucks, paper, minerals, and chemicals.

From the point of view of the banks the action would force the banks to recognize losses, possibly very large ones. The debtor countries would insist on settling claims at less than 100 cents per dollar of debt. Otherwise they would have no incentive to abandon the present following of piling loan upon loan in hopes that, someday, they will not have to borrow, just to pay interest. The size of losses that banks would have to accept could be settled only in negotiations between them and the debtors. Meltzer's very rough estimate is that it might take write-offs of 20% to 30% of the face value of the loans if the obligations of problem countries were reduced to market value. That could wipe out about one third of the capital of some of the largest US banks. But write-offs of that magnitude need not topple the banking system.

Moreover, Meltzer stresses, it is important to keep in mind that the bank already have sustained these losses; they just haven't admitted them. If the debtor countries repay some loans as described above, the actual value of the banks' losses should decline. The exchange would demonstrate to the world that the countries intend to honour their guarantees and the value of the remaining loans would rise. The banks might look weaker but they would be stronger.

The central argument made against this scheme is that it is impracticable, that developing countries would never surrender their patrimony to a bunch of foreign bankers. Giving up valuable resources to pay off foreign loans could be political suicide, but Meltzer believes it might not. For one thing many countries already permit private investment in state-owned enterprises. Some of the largest creditor banks have big equity positions in Third World countries.[8]

Two arguments can be put forward in favour of Meltzer's plan. Firstly, debtors and creditors share the losses; the claims become marketable and the creditors acquire an interest in the efficiency of the debtor countries. Secondly, it may well be better than some of the alternatives.

[8] In March 1985 Mexico announced that it was proposing letting foreign banks swap some of their loans to Mexican government companies for partial ownership in key government enterprises. Some creditor banks received a draft list of nearly forty companies being considered for debt to equity swaps, including some strategic state-owned enterprises that produce steel, trucks, paper, minerals and chemicals.

J. Guttentag and R. Herring

Guttentag and Herring outline a six part proposal with three short-term and three long-term proposals. Their proposals are:

- New marketable consol certificates with prior claim are issued. These certificates would be used to produce new loans to debtor countries by the IMF. They would have a prior claim on all other loans to that country, encouraging people to lend, knowing they are first in the queue for repayment. These certificates would have no maturity date so the debt-service would now only be one of interest payment and thereby reducing the cash flow problem. Countries may be more willing to accept this sort of stablilization programme under the control of the IMF if they knew that these loans continue to arrive.
- Turn old government debt into consol certificates. Again, new loans would take the form of certificates with no repayment dates. However, as this is not how money was first borrowed, the debtor country would have to pay a penalty rate.

One advantage of both these certificates is that they would be denominated in the currency of the debtor country and would consequently become less of a burden with inflation rather than more.

- Valuation of old debt. Regardless whether a country turns its old debt into consol certificates or not, it is proposed that the old debt remains at face value if the country keeps up to date with its payments. If, however, they do not, for every month that they are delinquent the value in the banks' books would be written down 1% (therefore written off in 100 months). The aim is slowly to write off the debt, cushioning the banks.

Proposals for long run aim reform to establish a mechanism that constrains the banks and the country before the levels of lending are excessive. Therefore, all loans should be periodically marked to market, i.e. valued at market rates. There are two problems with this. Firstly, it needs to be effective and, secondly, it will be difficult owing to the lack of a reliable market valuation rate. The aim is to speed up the rate at which problems are recognized. The proposal helps the banks to see their spreads and stiffens their negotiating stance.

Secondly a secondary market would have to be created. This secondary market would consist of people who deal in loans, i.e. IMF etc., buying loans and pooling them, then selling off participation. The aim is diversification of lending and to provide a mechanism for allowing the revaluation of the loans.

Thirdly there would have to be the disclosing detailed information on country exposure by individual banks to permit bank creditors to monitor such risks. This proposal allows some form of constraint to then be applied to the spread of any country's risk.

So the banks would be forced to mark the market – the foreign loans on their books, making banks more cautious about foreign lending. They could sell off loans at a market rate to the IMF, the World Bank, or a new entity, which would combine them with similar loans of other banks and would resell to the public participations in the pool (in a manner similar to the Federal Home Loan Mortgage Corporation in the United States). Countries in difficulty could convert their loans to consols (where principal is never repaid) at market interest rates. If they missed interest payments, the value of the loan would be marked down in the banks' book by 1% for each month's interest missed.

However, as Cline has pointed out, it is unclear why banks voluntarily would sell off sovereign loans at a deep discount as long as chances remained for greater recovery.[9] And in the absence of a wide market for such sales, it would be arbitrary for regulators to impose a low market valuation to which these assets would be marked. As for converting country loans to consols, it is unclear why countries should be given an infinite leash, even if the typical rescheduling leash of one to two years is too short.

Proposals affecting interest

The importance of interest costs for debtor countries

A glance at Table 10.1 illustrates the importance of changes in US interest rates on debtor countries. A rise of one percentage point in dollar interest rates increases Brazil's annual interest bill to its bankers by around $580 million – 3.6% of its projected imports for 1984. Mexican officials complain that the 1.50% rise in prime rates of American commercial banks early in 1984 offset virtually all the $1 billion increase in their non-traditional exports, so painfully achieved in 1983. Indeed a 1% rise in interest rates wipes out Mexico's tourist earnings for a year.

[9] W. R. Cline, "International Debt and the Stability of the World Economy" (Institute for International Economics, Sept. 1983).

Table 10.1. How a 1% Rise in Interest Rates
Affects Debtor Countries

	Increased interest payments of banks* ($m)	Projected 1984 imports ($ billion)	Cutback in imports needed to compensate ($ +)
Argentina	187	4.7	4.0
Brazil	85	16.0	3.6
Chile	521	3.3	2.6
Mexico	521	10.0	5.2
Peru	30	2.7	1.1
Venezuela	133	9.0	1.5

* Based on net debt at June, 1983
\+ Assuming exports stay unchanged

Source: *Bank for International Settlements* official figures

The most widely accepted estimates that each 1% fall (rise) in interest rates reduces (increases) debt payments by $US4 billion. Various schemes have been put forward to alleviate the impact of interest rate increases on debtor countries.

Interest rate capping

Interest rate capping is better described as a form of automatic rescheduling. The way it works is as follows. Assume all sides agree (and this is a hopeful assumption) that interest payment should not rise beyond 10% on LDC debt, but then that all market interest rates rise to, say, 11%. The banks then have to fund their deposits at 11%, but are only receiving 10% on their LDC assets. Essentially, unless in the likely event of an outside body giving the banks money, the banks' cash flow will be reduced. It is estimated that, for every 1% difference between the cap and market rate, the large nine money centre banks will lose around 9 to 10% of their net cash flow. The figures are therefore quite dramatic. Further, there are many different versions of capping and how it should be treated in the balance sheets of the banks.

Under one version we assume that the difference is not just lost, i.e. Latin America refusing to pay for the cap at some later date. If it does so refuse, this would essentially amount to default under any sensible banking rules. The question is, therefore, how to amortise the loan. The simplest way is to do just that, add the difference in interest to the life of the loan as capital repayments (i.e. the interest is capitalized). In this system the country is automatically rescheduling.

By this process banks would agree to reschedule a country's debt for thirty years. For the first ten years this would involve a conventional rescheduling except that part of the interest due might be capitalized or added to the rescheduled debt instead of being paid each year. After ten years the debt would convert into a twenty-year floating rate note which banks could sell if they wanted. If the debtor country was well on the way to recovery by then there should be no trouble selling the debt in the marketplace. If not, it would fall to a steep discount and banks would face losses. But at least they would have had ten years to make provisions for such losses in their balance sheets.

Debtors for their part would not have to worry about final repayment for thirty years, but they would have an incentive to adjust their economies before that. If they failed, their debt would fall to a discount when it became marketable, creditors would make losses and the borrowers' credit rating would again seriously be impaired.

Another version is to set up a special reserve account which is credited with the interest difference when the market rate is above the cap. If market rate then falls below the cap at a later date, the cap would remain and the difference be automatically used to pay off the reserve account. This scheme is currently very popular.

Paraguay – the first rate capping case

The World Bank is adopting one version of interest rate capping whereby there is a ceiling on the amount of interest a debtor has to pay in any one year. Interest payments are excused if market rates go above this ceiling but the debtor has to pay up later when they drop.

In June 1984 the World Bank announced a new $15 million co-financing loan for Paraguay, the proceeds of which are to be used to develop livestock farming. Bank officials say that, because this loan is very small, it should not be seen as some major new initiative on the debt crisis, but they expect it to be studied carefully by those government officials and banks that are still examining new mechanisms for dealing with the problem.

The loan itself is to be put together by a small group of banks led by Credit Agricole. It has a ten-year life and bears interest at a margin of 2.25% points over Euro-dollar rates for the first five years rising to 2.375% points thereafter. Repayments of principal begin after a grace period of five years.

For the first five years Paraguay will pay interest on the loan at the full market rate. After that, payment of principal and interest combined have been pre-set at $3.8m a year. This would allow the loan to be fully paid off after ten years if the interest charge, including the margin, does not exceed 12%.

If the interest charge turns out to be higher, the life of the loan will simply be increased (rather on the same principle under which the life of the mortgage can be extended to offset rises in interest rates), but after ten years the World Bank will lend Paraguay the outstanding balance so that the bank lenders can be repaid. It has also already agreed to guarantee service payments during the tenth year of the loan so that its maturity could be extended from the nine years originally offered by the banks.

In this way Paraguay is receiving partial protection from the effect on its cash flow of any increase in interest rates during the last five years of the loan's life.

The World Bank has been empowered by its board to offer such protection in its co-financing schemes since January of 1984, but this is the first time it has put the mechanism into effect. Officials say it would like to develop the technique further.

The Economist plan

The IMF has long had a compensatory financing facility (CFF) that makes loans to commodity exporters if their foreign exchange earnings fall because of factors beyond their control – a slump in world sugar prices, say, or frost in the coffee bushes. Yet high American interest rates have gouged much more out of the export earnings of some big borrowers than commodity mishaps have done.

As these high interest rates are caused by large US budget deficits it is suggested by *The Economist* that America could make some amends by supporting the establishment of a special interest rate compensatory facility in the IMF, similar to the successful commodity one, to help Latin America meet the extra $1.6 billion a year it has to pay to banks every time interest rates in New York rise by 1%. If commodity prices fall, poor exporters then have the right to draw more from them than the IMF; if world interest rates rise, poor debtors should also have the right. Disbursements of funds need not require conditionality. However, the moral hazard of all compensatory finance would still apply.

The Hudson Institute plan

The Hudson Institute suggests interest rates might be fixed in real terms while principal repayments increase in line with inflation. This would reduce interest service in the early years of a loan and increase principal repayments in later years. Such a reloading of loans could help debtors match their revenue flows to their financing obligations more closely.

Chapter 11
The Future

We have stressed throughout the book that the international debt crisis did not descend suddenly and will not disappear in the near future. It is to the reformation of existing international monetary and financial arrangements and agreements that we must look if the worst case scenarios of default and debt repudiation are to be avoided and a smooth adjustment to a more orderly game is to be found. Before making some concluding remarks about the outlook, it is worth recapitulating some of the major errors and lessons from the past.

International debt problems were caused, to a significant extent, by domestic policy failures in creditor *and* debtor countries. A favourable outlook for world output and trade remains, of course, crucial for a sustained improvement but lasting fiscal and monetary discipline remains just as indispensable if creditworthiness is to be restored and if desperately needed economic growth in a number of borrowing countries is to resume on a solid and credible foundation. We shall return to this subject in due course. Shortcomings in economic management need to be rectified to ensure that the proceeds of foreign borrowing are used productively. That foreign borrowing in some countries can be traced to the sustaining of consumption, capital flight and poorly managed investments, is sufficient to warn about the need for caution by both creditor and debtor.

Even where productive investment occurred, it is clear that economic policy adjustments were neither significant nor prompt enough.

The level of borrowing after the mid-to late-1970s by many LDCs exceeded their capacity to absorb capital productively, as a

189

consequence of which investment either failed to rise, or fell. As we described in earlier chapters Professor Bill Cline has estimated that of the $500 billion rise in LDC debt between 1973 and 1981, about $260 billion was attributable to the oil price rises, $100 billion to the 1981-1982 economic recession and $40 billion to the rise in real interest rates. There was, therefore, little left over for the purpose of productive investment, especially in countries where there was substantial capital flight in the early 1980s. Thus, foreign borrowing was too small to generate a growth in the stock of capital from which debt could be serviced with a net gain, or at least no net burden to, borrowers.

The point is that debtor governments could have, and should have, adjusted their policies much sooner to the external shocks that occurred from 1973 to 1982. When there is doubt about the duration and intensity of an internal shock (e.g. a rapid rise in the money supply) or an external shock (such as the OPEC price increases) policymakers in borrowing countries should take action more promptly to adjust the balance of payments (by some combination of devaluation, deflation, controls etc.) rather than by continuous financing (largely by borrowing). Recent history shows that in the past there was a tendency towards the latter. Borrowers and lenders generally expected all investments in borrowing countries – financed by capital raised abroad – to generate a true economic return; a stable or falling exchange value of the US dollar; stable or falling nominal and real interest rates and a continuation of normal world economic growth. None of these assumptions, however, were fulfilled after 1979. The problems posed by international debt are thus clearly linked to the tremendous gap that separated overly optimistic expectations from a rather more sober economic reality.

All forms of non-debt creating capital inflows should receive renewed attention. This is because such flows represent less financial risk for the receiving country, and also because the transfer of managerial skills and technical knowledge are normally associated with most forms of foreign direct investment.

Direct investment is perhaps the most important of such flows, even though its contribution to the financing of the deficits of the developing countries over the past decade has been only a quarter that of bank lending. Many developing countries have been unenthusiastic about inward direct investment, perhaps principally because – unlike bank borrowing – it involves a degree of direct control over domestic resources by foreign interests.

The most frequently encountered limitation on foreign investment is the degree of the percentage of ownership or the prohibition of the takeover of existing local firms. There are in some countries restrictions on the transfer of dividends or royalties. There are some countries which impose specific performance obligations. Moreover, it is rare for a foreign-owned firm to have unrestricted access to the host country's domestic savings or capital market.

Borrowing nations will need to set these political challenges against the constraints inherent in bank borrowing, especially involving the IMF, viz normally the need to follow restrained economic policies which maintain or restore creditworthiness.

The main advantages of direct investment are that it encourages the dissemination of managerial and technical skills. Furthermore, there are no remaining financial obligations if a project should fail: there is a financial exchange cost to the host country only when the investment is productive and profits are remitted abroad – and in these circumstances the project itself may well be generating or saving foreign exchange. If the project succeeds, the investor is likely to wish to maintain his investment, and not to repatriate it.

Since many bank lending decisions were made on the basis of erroneous assumptions or inadequate information, every effort designed to improve the volume and quality of information about project feasibility, economic conditions in debtor countries and bank exposures, deserves a high priority. The Institute of International Finance in Washington D.C., for example, now provides a valuable service, particularly to smaller banks, which might have helped to temper overenthusiastic lending decisions in past years. The central banks and supervisory authorities in major creditor countries are now gathering more information about banks' lending positions and scrutinising them more closely.

Borrowing countries must pay greater attention to suitable hedging policies against foreign exchange and interest rate risks. A balanced currency diversification of the debt portfolio, combined with a carefully designed approach to the problem of managing interest rate risk, will go a long way towards preventing unpleasant financial surprises.

Governments of lending countries should endeavour to pursue enlightened and broadly-based economic policies when dealing with debtor countries. This implies, firstly, that export credit guarantees should not be misused to boost domestic output and employment, even though the chances of serious and sustained debt service by foreign borrowers appear to be remote and, secondly, that governments should make every effort possible to provide private sector entities with comprehensive and current information about the macro-economic position and outlook of an individual debtor country. Particular attention should be paid to cross-border capital flows and the evolution of public sector debt.

Borrowing countries should be persuaded that, in the long run, so-called conservative, i.e. non-inflationary, fiscal and monetary policies do entail a real economic reward. Ultimately, the creditworthiness of a debtor country is at stake; and if that country is truly creditworthy, current account deficits are normally of little concern.

For every borrowing country now soliciting IMF – type financing, a meaningful objective should be to secure adequate external financing in private financial markets. Such an objective is by no means beyond the reach of many borrowing countries. Serious long-run economic policies do not depend on the availability of natural resources such as oil. As we showed in earlier chapters the experience of quite a few developed countries goes to show that natural resource availability is by no means a necessary or sufficient condition to create, over time, a sustained process of wealth accumulation.

Finally, the important lessons of the 1930s must not be forgotten. If private market operators, influenced or constrained by their respective governments to an undue extent, and creditor governments simultaneously:

- refuse to increase, or at least maintain, their purchases of non-subsidized goods from borrowing countries;
- refuse to discuss the long-term rescheduling of outstanding external debt; and
- refuse to provide more finance or insist on a reduction of the volume of outstanding credits,
  then the adjustment effort required to ensure normal debt service might exceed politically and socially acceptable limits in the borrowing countries.

Debt Reschedulings

The debt rescheduling of 1982-1983 may contain the seeds of new problems in the late 1980s. A number of debtor governments will face principal payments obligations that will be at least as onerous as those of 1982-1983, which proved to be excessive. As a result, the debt crisis for many nations will continue for several years unless there is early and lasting relief for LDCs in respect of lower interest rates and greater export opportunities. The more favourable global economic climate in 1984-1985 needs to be sustained and improved. In its absence, the financial obligations and reschedulings of debtor governments will continue to inhibit economic recovery and at the same time, renewed debt service problems may again threaten the rebuilding of banks' capital positions. In the worst case the debt situation may continue until a resolution is "forced" by a major shock, provided perhaps by necessary major bank failures, political and economic upheavals in major debtor nations or a sharp financial contraction in creditor nations.

Table 11.1. Long-Term Debt Principal Repayments*
($ billion)

	1982	1983	1984	1985	1986	1987	1988
Argentina	1.3	1.5	1.5	1.5	3.9	3.6	1.4
Brazil	4.7	4.7	5.8	6.9	8.1	8.2	8.0
Chile	0.7	0.5	0.5	0.6	0.9	0.8	8.0
Mexico	4.3	8.9	5.7	5.9	7.2	8.0	4.9
Venezuela	1.3	1.7	2.3	2.1	2.1	2.0	1.1
Excess(+)/Shortfall(−) Re: scheduled payments as at end 1981:	−2.2	+5.9	+4.1	+5.9	+12.4	+12.3	+8.4

* Projections at end 1982 except for 1982 data which was previous year's overstated projection

Source: *World Bank, World Debt Tables*

The payments due in 1986-1987 as can be seen from Table 11.1 are over twice as high as those made in 1982 and note that, for Mexico, where the debt crisis came alive in 1982, principal payments will be $8 billion in 1987 compared with less than $4.5 billion. Without a sustained improvement in the external environment, some countries will not be able to repay as scheduled. There must clearly be limits to the extent that debtor countries will go on reducing imports and living standards as the price for continued access to foreign savings. The limits may not be reached in debtor nations which can continue to record reasonably strong economic growth. Since this will or ought to be based on buoyant export performance, a favourable external environment is essential.

The debt game and the international economy

It is now thought, that if economic growth in industrial countries of 2.5% per year can be sustained through the 1980's, that debt ratios can be reduced to acceptable levels. This scenario provides also for the continued expansion of world trade and for the reversal of the tendency towards greater protectionism since this threatens directly the ability of debtor countries to earn foreign exchange with which to service debt.

The immediate implications for the governments of creditor countries are to adopt or continue with economic policies that create confidence in sustained expansion. The most important policy objectives, therefore, should be to keep inflation low through appropriate monetary policies and to stimulate investment, especially in modern sectors of industry, through the flexible use of budgetary policies and tax and spending policies to encourage investment, innovation and incentives. The biggest threat to sustained economic expansion in industrial countries is probably the risk of recession in the United States. Whilst a number of factors might contribute to an increase in this risk, one of the most important is the size of US budget deficit and, as a result, the US balance of payments deficit. The prospects for sustained, strong growth in the US would be enhanced by a credible strategy to reduce substantially the deficit over the next few years.

The implications for the governments of debtor countries are that they should adopt or sustain policies that achieve a growth in exports of the order of 5-6% per year – about the same or a little higher than the desired growth in world trade. Debtor nations will, however, have to persevere with adjustment policies for a considerable period. The standard IMF menu would require countries to reduce inflation and the rates of fiscal and monetary expansion; to phase out price distortions and impediments; to allow exchange rates, prices and interest rates to adjust freely and promptly; and to reduce barriers and restrictions on trade and competition. Not all countries may find these policies socially or politically palatable, especially over a number of years. Therefore, the more favourable is the foreign environment, the easier it will be for countries to implement these adjustment policies and spread the costs and burdens over time.

Progress to date has been remarkable, at least in the major debtor countries. Both Mexico and Brazil recorded large trade surpluses in 1984, albeit at the cost of higher inflation. The fact that smaller debtors such as Peru, Sudan and Bolivia show few signs of economic recuperation despite three years of IMF supervision and austerity is of concern locally but less so both in a global context and from the banks' viewpoint. The distinguishing key to the successes recorded by Mexico and Brazil is their significant economic flexibility – a point that may be applied to some Asian LDCs that never ran into debt-service difficulties (e.g. South Korea, Taiwan, Singapore). Indeed, in 1985, both Mexico and Brazil are expected to see an improvement in economic growth for the first time this decade. The obvious gain is that economic growth enhances the willingness to service debt on time and an improved trade performance enhances the ability to do so.

There are, inevitably, longer-term risks that need to be kept in mind. The first is inflation. The threat of inflation is its destabilizing impact from a political standpoint but, more importantly, its potential repercussions in undermining economic performance overall. The second is the generation of large trade surpluses. These have resulted from a massive switch of resources from domestic demand to the export and import substitute sectors – a process that tends to fuel domestic inflation, for example, as a result of currency devaluation and the abolition of subsidies on fuels and foreign food imports, while the erection of import barriers creates shortages and stifles competition.

Arguably, therefore, debtor nations have not really resolved the problems of generating export surpluses to satisfy their creditors and of stimulating domestic economic recovery except as a result of allowing higher inflation. More adjustment efforts need to be pursued with regard to reducing domestic spending, especially on consumption. However, this may not be acceptable in some countries, except over very short periods. In any event, we have to ask whether a policy of running sustained large trade surpluses can be a permanent solution to the debt problem, given the costs involved. By way of example, from 1983 to 1992, Brazil's trade surplus will have to average around 4% GNP – and Mexico, 7% GNP – if interest payments are to be met fully and on time without much, if any, new borrowing. Compare these figures with the greatest export machine in post-Second World War economic history – Japan, which recorded a trade surplus of 3% GNP in 1984.

Against such a volatile and tenuous background, it is easy to see why a sustained expansion in economic growth and world trade is so vital to a permanent resolution of the debt game and how threatening are the prospects of a new recession, increasing protectionism and sudden lurches towards expansionary policies in debtor nations. The far-reaching implications of the international debt game for the world economy will continue to hang in the balance for the forseeable future. We can only hope that time and orderly economic conditions will allow the game to be played properly according to the rules and not be interrupted by a new financial shock or by a rogue player.

Index